Germanicus, Rome's Unlucky Prince

To my family, old and new

Germanicus, Rome's Unlucky Prince

Death, Trial, Memory

Alessio Perry

Pen & Sword
MILITARY

First published in Great Britain in 2025 by
Pen & Sword Military
An imprint of
Pen & Sword Books Ltd
Yorkshire – Philadelphia

ISBN 978 1 03612 840 1

A CIP catalogue record for this book is available from the British Library.

Typeset by Simon and Sons ITES Services Private Limited
Printed and bound in the UK by CPI Group (UK) Ltd, Croydon, CR0 4YY.

The Publisher's authorised representative in the EU for product safety is Authorised Rep Compliance Ltd., Ground Floor, 71 Lower Baggot Street, Dublin D02 P593, Ireland.
www.arccompliance.com

For a complete list of Pen & Sword titles please contact

PEN & SWORD BOOKS LIMITED
47 Church Street, Barnsley, South Yorkshire, S70 2AS, England
E-mail: enquiries@pen-and-sword.co.uk
Website: www.pen-and-sword.co.uk
or
PEN AND SWORD BOOKS
1950 Lawrence Road, Havertown, PA 19083, USA
E-mail: uspen-and-sword@casematepublishers.com
Website: www.penandswordbooks.com

Contents

Illustrations and Maps

Maps

Key Chronology

31 BCE	Battle of Actium between Octavian and Mark Antony
30 BCE	Octavian enters Alexandria, Egypt; Mark Antony and Cleopatra commit suicide; end of civil wars
27 BCE	Octavian is given the honorific title of 'Augustus'; scholars tend to see this event as the beginning of the 'empire'
16–15 BCE	Birth of Germanicus, to Drusus the Elder and Antonia
14 BCE	Birth of Agrippina
9 BCE	Death of Drusus the Elder, Germanicus' father
2 BCE	Julia the Elder, Augustus' only daughter, conspires against her father to have him removed; she is exiled to the island of Pandataria, in the Tyrrhenian Sea
1 BCE	Germanicus comes of age
4 CE	Augustus formally adopts his grandson Agrippa Postumus and his stepson Tiberius as his heirs; Tiberius is in turn asked to formally adopt Germanicus
4 or 5 CE	Germanicus marries Agrippina, Augustus' granddaughter
6 CE	Birth of Nero Caesar, Germanicus' eldest son; Agrippa Postumus is banished
7–9 CE	Germanicus is in Illyria campaigning under Tiberius; birth of Germanicus' second son, Drusus Caesar
9 CE	Disaster of Teutoburg at the hands of Arminius; Augustus appoints Germanicus to oversee the Rhine frontier
10–11 CE	Germanicus is on the Rhine under the command of his uncle Tiberius
12 CE	Birth of Germanicus' third son, Gaius Caesar (Caligula); Germanicus becomes consul in Rome for the first time

13 CE	Germanicus is made *legatus Augusti pro praetore* over Gaul by Augustus; he possibly quelled an insurrection in Gaul at this time
14 CE	Germanicus is still in Gaul, making preparations for a military campaign beyond the Rhine; deaths, in quick succession, of Augustus, Agrippa Postumus and Julia the Elder; Tiberius becomes the new *princeps*; Germanicus is given *imperium maius proconsulare*; legionary revolts on the Rhine and in Pannonia; Germanicus leads a punitive expedition against the Marsi and the Bructeri beyond the Rhine
15 CE	New expedition beyond the Rhine into Germania; Germanicus oversees the erection of the monument to the fallen of Teutoburg; birth of Germanicus' eldest daughter, Agrippina the Younger; Sejanus becomes praetorian prefect
16 CE	Battle of Idistavisus; battle of the Vallum of the Angrivarii; Arminius is contained
17 CE	Germanicus celebrates his triumph in Rome; he is granted the *imperium maius* over the eastern provinces of the empire and sets off; on the way, he visits his brother Drusus the Younger in Illyria and then Actium
18 CE	Germanicus competes in the chariot races at Olympia; he then visits Athens and Troy; he is appointed consul for the second time, to be held with Tiberius; Piso is appointed proconsul of Syria; settlement of Cappadocia; Germanicus crowns Zeno king of Armenia; meeting between Germanicus and the Parthian emissaries on the Euphrates; meeting with the Nabatean king
19 CE	Germanicus visits Egypt; after returning to Syria, he dies
20 CE	Germanicus' funeral in Rome and grant of posthumous honours; Piso and Plancina's trial
23 CE	Death of Drusus the Younger, Tiberius' biological son
26 CE	Tiberius withdraws from Rome to the island of Capri
29 CE	Death of Livia Augusta; the showdown between Agrippina and Sejanus begins

30 CE	Agrippina and Nero Caesar are exiled
31 CE	Fall of Sejanus from power and death; death of Nero Caesar
33 CE	Death of Agrippina, of her son Drusus Caesar and of Plancina
37 CE	Death of Tiberius and of Antonia, Germanicus' mother; Caligula becomes emperor
39 CE	Caligula's northern expedition
41 CE	Assassination of Caligula; Claudius, Germanicus' brother, becomes emperor
49 CE	Agrippina the Younger, Germanicus' daughter, marries Claudius
51 CE	Nero, Agrippina the Younger's only son, is formally adopted by Claudius
54 CE	Death of Claudius; Nero becomes emperor
59 CE	Nero has his mother Agrippina the Younger killed
68 CE	Suicide of Nero; end of Julio-Claudian rule

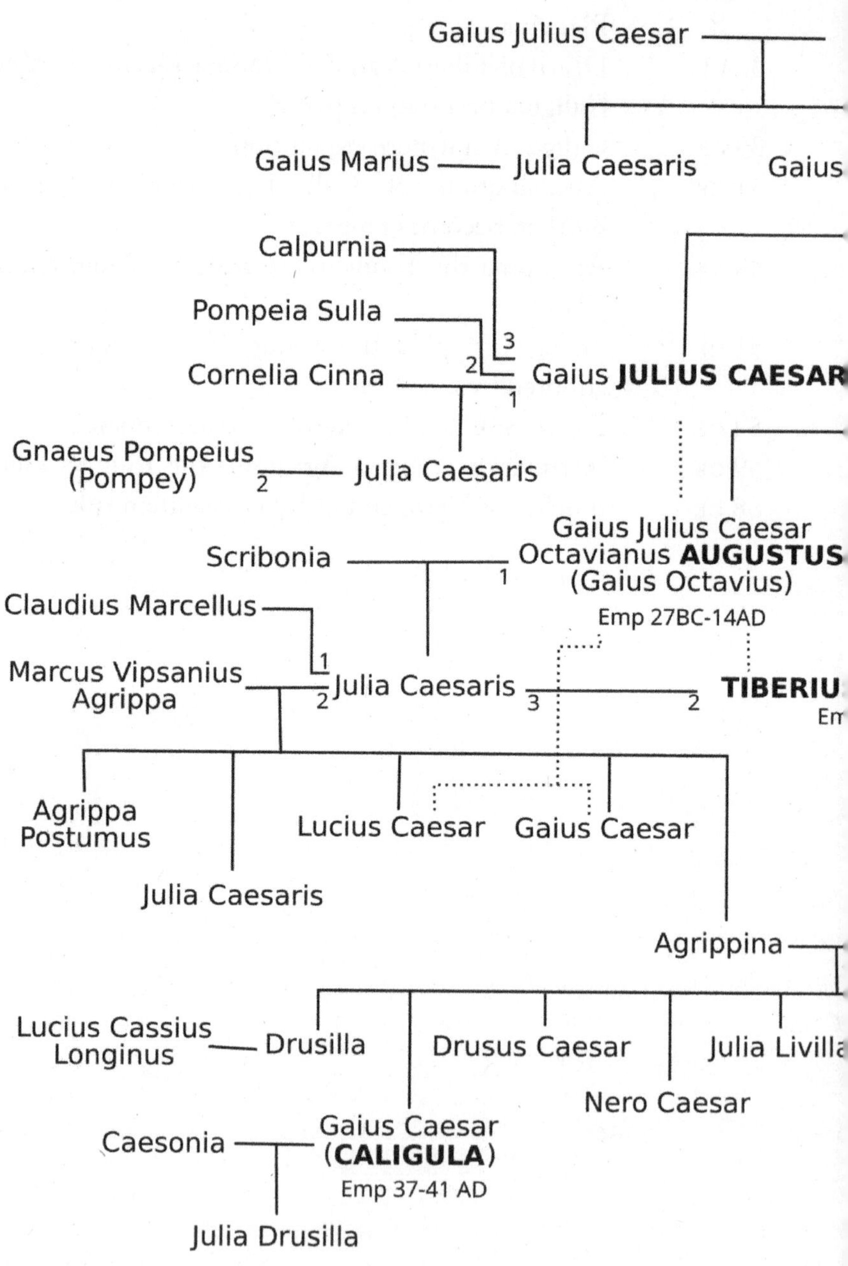

Julio-Claudi
Gaius Julius Caesar
Gaius Marius
Julia Caesaris
Gaius
Calpurnia
Pompeia Sulla
Cornelia Cinna
3
2
1
Gaius JULIUS CAESAR
Gnaeus Pompeius (Pompey)
2
Julia Caesaris
Gaius Julius Caesar Octavianus AUGUSTUS (Gaius Octavius)
Emp 27BC-14AD
Scribonia
1
Claudius Marcellus
1
Marcus Vipsanius Agrippa
2
Julia Caesaris
3
2
TIBERIU
Em
Agrippa Postumus
Julia Caesaris
Lucius Caesar
Gaius Caesar
Agrippina
Lucius Cassius Longinus
Drusilla
Drusus Caesar
Julia Livilla
Nero Caesar
Caesonia
Gaius Caesar (CALIGULA)
Emp 37-41 AD
Julia Drusilla

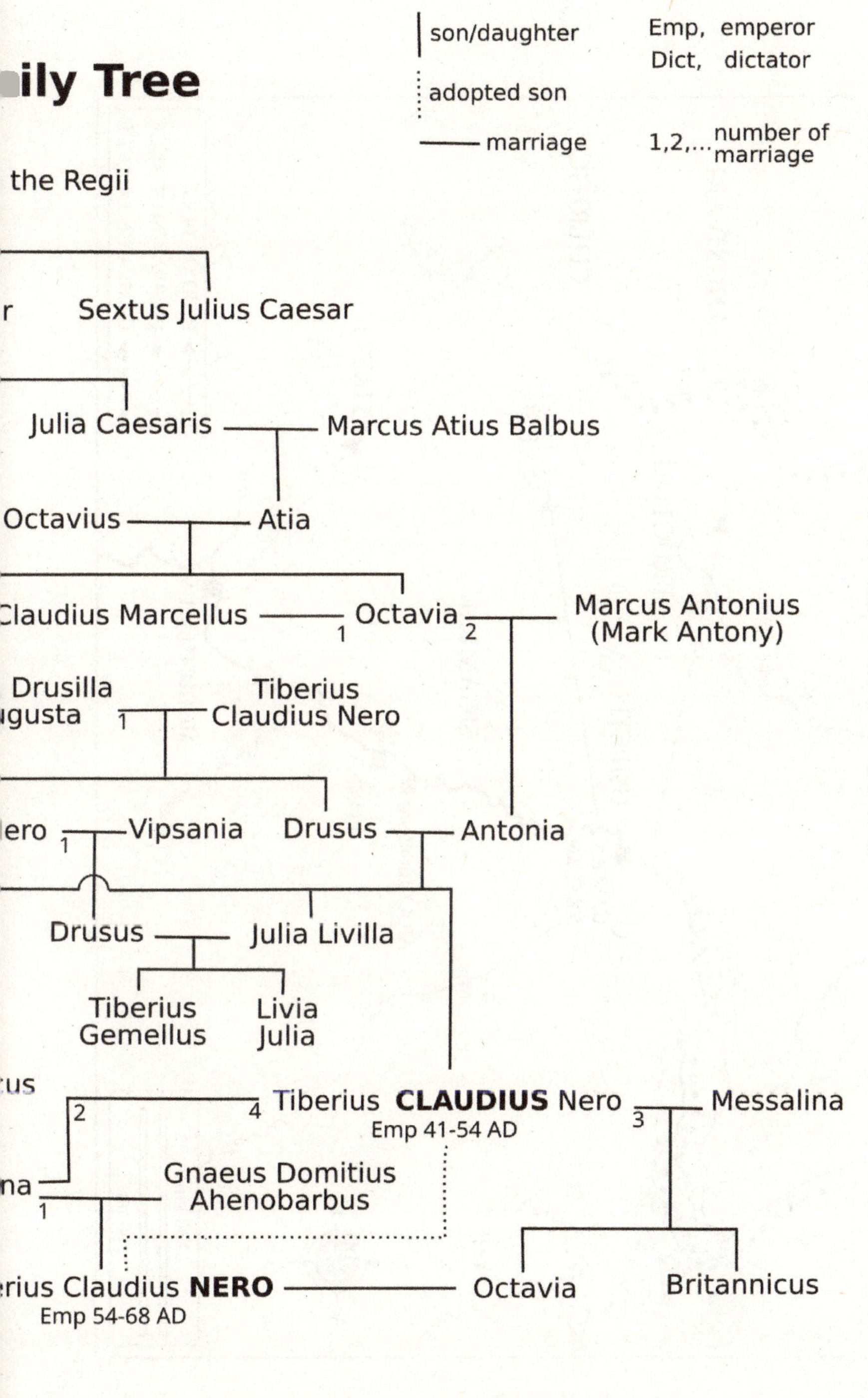
ily Tree
the Regii
son/daughter
adopted son
marriage
Emp, emperor
Dict, dictator
1,2,... number of marriage
r
Sextus Julius Caesar
Julia Caesaris
Marcus Atius Balbus
Octavius
Atia
Claudius Marcellus
1
Octavia
2
Marcus Antonius
(Mark Antony)
Drusilla
ugusta
1
Tiberius
Claudius Nero
ero
1
Vipsania
Drusus
Antonia
Drusus
Julia Livilla
Tiberius
Gemellus
Livia
Julia
us
2
4
Tiberius CLAUDIUS Nero
Emp 41-54 AD
3
Messalina
na
1
Gnaeus Domitius
Ahenobarbus
rius Claudius NERO
Emp 54-68 AD
Octavia
Britannicus

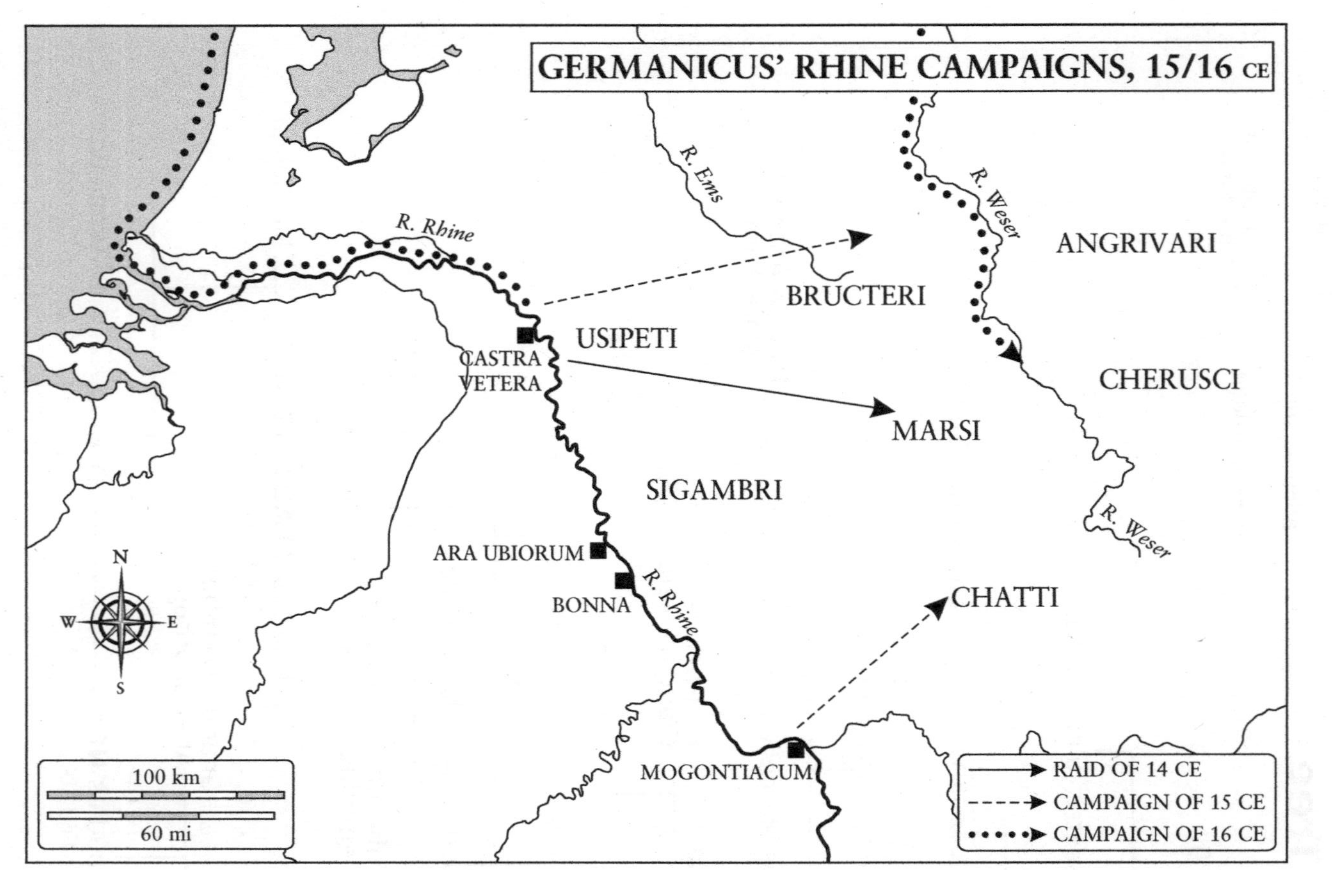
GERMANICUS' RHINE CAMPAIGNS, 15/16 CE
R. Ems
R. Weser
ANGRIVARI
R. Rhine
BRUCTERI
USIPETI
CASTRA VETERA
CHERUSCI
MARSI
SIGAMBRI
R. Weser
N
W
E
S
ARA UBIORUM
BONNA
R. Rhine
CHATTI
MOGONTIACUM
100 km
60 mi
RAID OF 14 CE
CAMPAIGN OF 15 CE
CAMPAIGN OF 16 CE

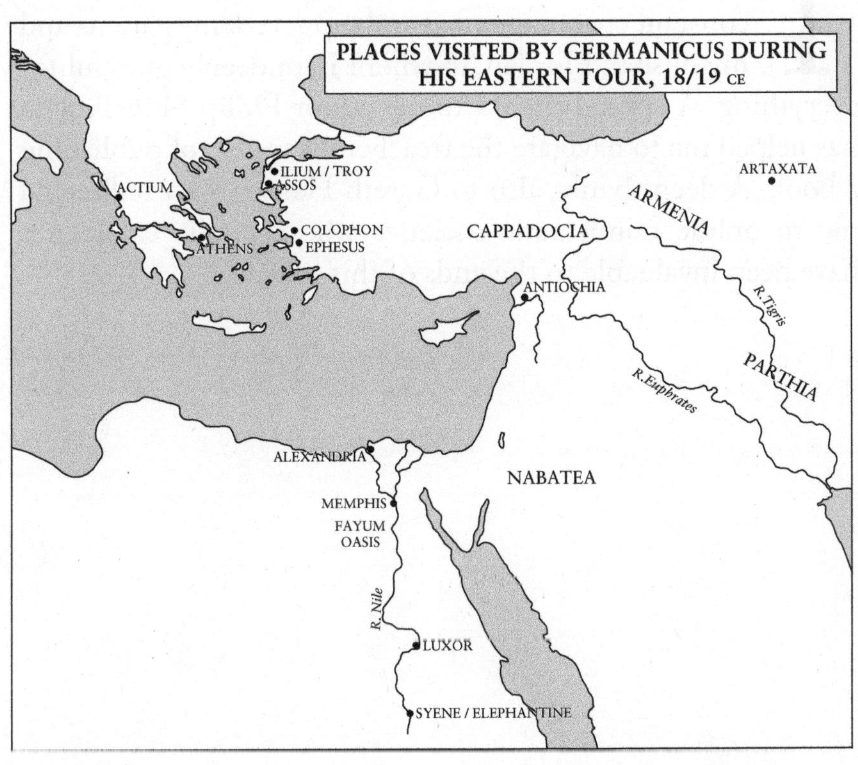
PLACES VISITED BY GERMANICUS DURING HIS EASTERN TOUR, 18/19 CE
ILIUM / TROY
ASSOS
ACTIUM
COLOPHON
ATHENS
EPHESUS
CAPPADOCIA
ARTAXATA
ARMENIA
ANTIOCHIA
R. Tigris
PARTHIA
R. Euphrates
ALEXANDRIA
NABATEA
MEMPHIS
FAYUM OASIS
R. Nile
LUXOR
SYENE / ELEPHANTINE

Acknowledgements

This book would have not seen the light without the constant encouragement and support of my parents and my husband Jordan, to whom I am deeply grateful for everything. A special thanks to my editor Philip Sidnell, who has helped me to navigate the treacherous waters of publishing a book. A deep thanks also to Gareth Harney who redirected me to online numismatic societies whose public catalogues have been invaluable to the ends of this research.

Introduction

You may wonder, reader, why, out of so many attributes one could choose, I decided to call this young prince unlucky. Among the many epithets associated with royalty, unlucky is not one that tends to rank on top. At first glance, this could have been the case for our protagonist too. After all, Germanicus, nephew of the emperor Tiberius, grandnephew of the 'founder' of the Roman empire Augustus, seemed to possess all that a Roman man could have possibly desired – beauty, strength, virtue, education, a devoted and chaste wife, numerous offspring, illustrious ancestors, a brilliant career and the prospect of inheriting the throne of the mightiest state of antiquity. Until the Blind Goddess decided to turn her gaze elsewhere.

For Germanicus died suddenly in 19 CE, aged only 33, leaving the Roman world in a state of shock. While his body was still warm, rumours about murder by poison were already spreading like wildfire. Along with them went mentions of an uncle and a grandmother who, out of fear and jealousy, may have made sure that the popular young man was removed from the scene before he could jeopardize their position. But was it really so? Where does the boundary between fact and rumour lie? Can a kernel of truth be recovered, if anything at all?

This is not a linear and comprehensive biography of the man Germanicus, from beginning to end. For that, I redirect readers to the recent, exhaustive and comprehensive works of Lindsay Powell and Yann Rivière on the subject.[1] This book actually starts at the end, exploring first and foremost Germanicus' death. How much can we discern of what truly befell the young prince? Did he really die by poisoning or of natural causes? If he was murdered, who carried out the sacrilegious act? Was there someone behind the scenes who commissioned the murder to further their own goals?

In order to answer these questions – and to assess the veracity of the rumour that it had been Tiberius, Germanicus' biological uncle and stepfather, who had ordered his death – this book will explore what went on between the prince and the emperor. How much does their supposedly tense relationship correspond to the truth? Can we trust our literary sources wholeheartedly, or do we get a different picture if we analyse them together with other kinds of evidence? We will retrace some of the key moments of Germanicus' life to see how much of the relations between stepfather and stepson can be reconstructed. More in detail, we will assess Germanicus' time and role on the river Rhine, at the edge of the empire, soon after the emperor Augustus' death in 14 CE. We then follow him on his journey eastwards as representative of his stepfather, and stop with him in Egypt, a land to which the young prince allegedly fell victim as many others had done before (and since). We will discuss the battle of attrition he had with Piso, Tiberius' new and controversial governor of Syria, allegedly sent there to spy on Germanicus by the emperor himself. And we will see how Piso's wife, Plancina, may have played a bigger role than the one the sources credit her with. It is at this point that we will also meet Agrippina, Germanicus' indomitable wife. This book will be as much hers as his. The part she played both during her husband's life and after his death should not be underestimated; it is probably due to her and to their circle of friends that Germanicus' memory has been preserved in such a positive light.

Next, we will deal with the trial of Piso and Plancina for Germanicus' alleged murder once they came back to Rome. But were they tried purely as suspected killers? Or did these two people meet their fate because there were more pressing and concrete accusations against them?

Finally, we will see how Germanicus' life and memory were exploited by a series of individuals – his stepfather, his wife, his brother, and his offspring – in order to achieve their own personal, political aims. Based on this, how much of the 'true' Germanicus can we actually claim to know? We therefore conclude with our justification for the reference to this young star of the Roman world as an 'unlucky' prince.

Before beginning, I have provided you, my reader, with a note on the extant sources that I have used to reconstruct Germanicus' story. It is not an essential part of this book, but it may help to raise awareness about what kind of sources we are dealing with, and how mindful we must be when handling them. After this, there is a section which sets the stage for our story; you will find here some basic information about the background in which Germanicus was born and raised, up to the point of Augustus' death in 14 CE. This second section is aimed for those who may be unfamiliar with the topic at large or who may want to refresh their memory of the situation in Rome at the turn of the BCE and CE centuries.

While reading, you will also notice some paragraphs in a different style. These are what I call 'historical snapshots' – short paragraphs of fiction which I wrote on the basis of the extant sources. Their aim is to introduce the reader to feelings and ideas which the protagonists of our story might have had at certain points in their lives. With no claim to be offering them as anything but fiction, I hope they may assist in setting the tone for a better grasp and understanding of the events narrated in the book.

A note on our sources

The life of Germanicus can be roughly reconstructed from the combination of different kinds of sources – literary, epigraphic (inscriptions), papyrological, numismatic (coinage), and archaeological. Naturally, the literary and historical accounts are those which tend to take centre stage, but we will see how it is only thanks to their integration with other types of sources that a clearer, more reliable picture can be obtained.

When it comes to literary sources, we need first to remember that we do not possess original manuscripts and that the extant versions have been left to us by a succession of writers and compilers who felt the need to preserve these works. Naturally, in this act of rewriting we cannot be sure of how much might have been altered, lost, misunderstood or simply forgotten. Secondly, we need to be mindful that ancient authors – like those of today – were shaped by their cultural, political, and social background; all these elements underpinned their writings, playing a role in shaping the authors' agendas too. This does not mean that we should discard whatever has been left to us of course, but it is important to be aware that the authors were not infallible, objective voices of truth. In this section, we will examine the background, styles and literary agendas of the five most significant authors whose accounts preserve relevant information about Germanicus and his family.

We shall start with Tacitus, by many considered the ablest and most significant ancient Roman historian. His reputation is due both to his comprehensiveness in recording events and his skill in portraying characters which feel very much alive to a modern reader too. Tacitus, however, did not live at the time of Germanicus; in fact, we can place his literary activity between the end of the first and the beginning of the second centuries CE, during the reigns of the emperors Domitian, Nerva, and Trajan. Tacitus spent much of his early adulthood under the last Flavian emperor – a ruler not much loved by the senatorial order to which Tacitus belonged. This life experience may have shaped Tacitus' attitude and understanding towards the principate and may have contributed to his idea of what it meant to be a good *princeps*.[2] His negative attitude is generally reflected in Tacitus' portrayal of the Julio-Claudian emperors in the *Annals*.[3] Most interesting, nevertheless, is the author's account of the emperor Tiberius: he is described initially as a moderate ruler, who started degenerating morally after the death of Germanicus – as if the presence of the young prince had prevented the emperor's vices from coming out.

At the outset of the *Annals*, Tacitus claims to be interested in providing the reader with 'a truthful and impartial account' of the years after Augustus' death, wrapping the narrative in a moralistic tone typical of senatorial historiography. To give the author credit, Tacitus consulted and included a lot of archival material in his research – material which he could have easily accessed from the senatorial records. He also does admit, however, to having included in his work *rumores* when he thinks them to be relevant – though he is also honest in specifying when a claim is reported only as a rumour. Tacitus was highly skilful in combining these materials with a powerful, varied and tight writing style which has given him his well-deserved fame as the ablest Roman historian. He was able to create powerful characters and sketches which still dominate our understanding of some of the early Roman emperors.

In order to understand the way in which Tacitus worked, it is worth giving a couple of concrete examples – which hopefully will make the reader appreciate why we cannot take everything that an author says at face value. At the opening of Book 4 of his *Annals*, which begins the second trio of books dedicated to Tiberius, Tacitus brilliantly combines structural change with a shift in the emperor's rule: it is at this point that the flourishing of the imperial house and the good administration of the empire begin to be overtaken by a series of misfortunes and crimes, which ultimately lead to Sejanus' (Tiberius' praetorian prefect) ascendancy.[4] Another example deals with Tiberius' retreat to the isle of Capri in 26 CE (after which he never set foot in Rome again). Tacitus uses the geographical features of the island to depict the change in the emperor's character: Edwards describes how he draws on 'the insularity and the isolation of Capri to influence the reader's perception of Tiberius' retirement', which will be populated by savagery and debauchery.[5]

The portrayal of Germanicus does not escape a similar manipulation. Let's remind ourselves of how the young prince's death is said to have unleashed Tiberius' inner demons. Some authors would rather see Germanicus, as portrayed by Tacitus, more as an antithesis to the principate itself than to Tiberius as an individual; his openness and camaraderie are constantly opposed to Tiberius' dissimulation and vindictiveness, which are considered traits of the principate as an institution.[6] If this is truly the case, to what extent can we claim to know who the 'real' Germanicus was behind such skilful literary artifices? It is again thanks to the combination of more sources that a clearer answer can be gained.

Our second author is Suetonius, most famous for his much-quoted *Lives of the* [first] *Twelve Caesars*, from Caesar to Domitian. Suetonius was a near contemporary to Tacitus, achieving a high-ranking post in the administration of the emperor Hadrian. Unlike Tacitus however, he was not of noble background, being from the equestrian order – the *equites*. This social class had been strengthened by the reforms of the emperor Augustus, with many positions created exclusively for 'knights', as they were deemed more reliable and loyal to the *princeps* than the aristocratic senators. It was during his time in the employment of Hadrian that Suetonius accessed much of the material that later flowed into his *Lives*.

These so-called 'biographies' focus on the individual lives of the emperors – in complete contrast to traditional Roman historiography, which tended to narrate events year by year. Each life is structured around the opposition between its main character's virtues and vices.[7] Although this may appear rather simplistic at first, the author, in order to achieve such characterizations, often includes and discusses different versions of the same event – a factor which undeniably proves his value as a source.[8]

Suetonius' *Lives* make another perfect example to study the ways in which an author's social and cultural background may have shaped his own work. For instance, Suetonius tended to include details and anecdotes about his characters which the senatorial tradition would normally consider too 'low' to be recorded in a 'traditional' historical work. But he did so in order to give a more comprehensive picture of his characters and to achieve his moralistic purpose.[9]

Like Tacitus, Suetonius was capable of carefully arranging his material so as to reach a concluding judgement on his subject. This is very evident, for instance, in his portrait of Augustus as a merciful ruler. Suetonius wanted to convey the image of the first emperor as a clement leader, but he could not avoid narrating instances of his cruelty as well – such as the time when Augustus denied mercy to prisoners (who were fellow Roman citizens) after the battle of Perusia (present-day Perugia) in 40 BCE. In order not to discourage the reader from reaching his intended conclusion, the author simply placed these more 'controversial' actions in a broader context. He justified the reasons for which Augustus acted the way he did, ensuring such details would not affect his message of the emperor as a merciful individual.[10]

After Suetonius, we have Cassius Dio, who lived roughly two hundred years after the events of this book, between the end of the second century and the beginning of the third CE. Dio was a Greek from Bythinia, a region located in modern north-western Turkey, roughly opposite Istanbul. He, like Tacitus, was a senator from a noble local family and in his life he became quite close to the emperor Septimius Severus for a time. His *Roman History* narrates the events from the origins of Rome to his own era. Today his work has survived partially fragmented, although we are very lucky that the section dealing with Tiberius' reign has reached us almost intact.

In historian Marta Sordi's words, the greatest merit of Dio is not to have copied Tacitus when he could have easily done so.[11] Instead, Dio conducted his own research and included at times different versions of the same events; he was not a simple compiler, but also provided judgement and interpretation of the materials he decided to record.[12] In typical senatorial fashion, his portrayal of Augustus' descendants is generally negative – in the case of Tiberius, this may be due to the hostility of a specific, unidentified source contemporary to the events of our book, which was used not only by Dio, but by Tacitus and Suetonius too.[13] It is from this same source that the positive portrayal of Germanicus derives.

Previous scholars believed that Dio showed no political agenda in his compilation of the *History*.[14] New studies have however shed light on how the author's political and cultural background deeply shaped the composition and style of his work. More in particular, philologists Carsten Lange and Jesper Madsen have argued that Dio's entire history is centred on his vision of an idealized form of Roman monarchical government.[15] According to this idea, in his books dedicated to the individual emperors Dio developed a theory of what the best kind of monarchy is and of the typical problems that come with it.

It should be pretty clear then, that Dio was not a simple recorder of events. In fact, he even used to deconstruct official versions of facts promoted by less competent emperors. Thus, he turned these figures from 'bad' emperors into tyrants through the exploitation of clever literary devices.[16]

Yet probably the most intriguing author to be introduced in this section is Velleius Paterculus. In contrast with the three writers discussed above, Velleius lived at the time of the events of our book. Hence, one could be forgiven for thinking that his work would constitute a major source for the study of Germanicus. Unfortunately, the worth of Velleius' history in relation to the young prince is minimal. For instance, he does not even mention Germanicus' death. This is probably due to the nature of Velleius' work: this *trascursus* (a 'dash' through history) shows a practical, everyday usefulness in complete contrast to the moralizing tone and intent of the 'higher', senatorial type of historiography.[17]

This factor, however, possibly makes his work even more interesting, for it gives no hint of any existing friction between Tiberius and his stepson, nor is there any reported suspicion about Germanicus' death. This puts Velleius' history in complete contrast with the works of Tacitus, Suetonius, and Dio who, as already mentioned above, probably derived much of their material about this topic from a common source hostile to the emperor.

Velleius was a soldier and a *homo novus*,[18] who served in the army under Tiberius for many years, between 4 and 12 CE. We know that he even participated in Tiberius' triumph against the Germans in 13 CE. He was not an aristocrat and as a soldier he was one of many who benefited greatly from Augustus' new regime and from his reorganization of the army.[19] Because of this obvious connection with the principate in general, and with Tiberius in particular, scholars have generally received Velleius' work negatively. More specifically, the author was seen as servile at best and at worst wholly biased towards the emperor.[20] This negative interpretation has been challenged in recent times and a new generation of scholars has put Velleius' work into context, trying to understand the intention behind his writing.[21]

Again in contrast with Tacitus, Suetonius, and Dio, Velleius' characters are portrayed in a more nuanced way, rather than black-and-white figures.[22] Yet these characters often personify symbols and abstract ideas which go beyond their own historicity. This is the case with Tiberius, who becomes the absolute protagonist of the latter part of Velleius' work. The emperor is not simply worshipped in terms of personal adoration; to Velleius' mind, Tiberius encapsulates that typically Roman, Republican virtue which finds its continuation into the principate via this *princeps*.[23] Therefore, Velleius' account is not a simple panegyric: it is a work which reflects the ideas and times of the author and which places the emperor in the larger frame of Roman history.

There is something on which Tacitus, Suetonius, Dio, and Velleius all agree on, however: Tiberius' usual preference for moderation and mercy. But how can we reconcile these traits with the vile depiction of the emperor during his time on the island of Capri? This is precisely the reason why we need to be mindful of an author's agenda when we approach his work.

The final author we will be dealing with is Flavius Josephus. The *Jewish Antiquities*, among his many works, are particularly important for our purposes – in them we find information which is not found anywhere else.

Josephus was a Jewish noble who took part in the revolt against Rome between 66 and 70 CE. After Titus' destruction of Jerusalem in 70 CE, Josephus moved to Rome, where he became a close confidant and collaborator of the emperor Vespasian. His *Jewish Antiquities*, aimed at both a Jewish and non-Jewish elite, were written to demonstrate how God was ever watchful over human affairs, Jewish or not.[24]

Most interestingly, Josephus' is the most detailed account that we have dealing with Caligula's murder and Claudius' accession – the son and the brother of Germanicus, respectively. Josephus' work may have been influenced by that of his patron, Herod Agrippa II, who had had close ties with the household of Antonia, mother of Germanicus.[25] Such links are especially evident in the telling of Claudius' accession, for instance, where Herod Agrippa's role is highly inflated and definitely exaggerated. We thus need to be mindful of this clearly pro-Antonian background, which may have also affected the portrayal of Germanicus and of his family.

You would be very much forgiven, reader, if at this point a natural question comes to your mind: how can we trust these sources, after all that we have just discussed? Thankfully, these are not the only kind of materials that we can rely upon in reconstructing past events. There are other types of evidence which have the huge benefit of being contemporary and of having reached us directly from those times: inscriptions, papyri, coins, and archaeological remains. We need to be mindful of course, that all these objects were commissioned by people who themselves had an agenda and personal intentions. However, by combining and contrasting these types of evidence with each other and with the literary accounts, a clearer picture begins to emerge. It's this work of combination and integration which will help us to shed more light on Germanicus, his deeds, his relationships and his death.

Setting the Stage

To better understand Germanicus, we need to place him in his own context.[26] We shall thus give here a brief overview of the political situation and of his family up to 14 CE, the year of Augustus' death and Tiberius' access to the throne.

Octavian's defeat of Mark Antony and Cleopatra at Actium, followed by the couple's suicide in 30 BCE, brought to an end a long period of civil strife in Rome. In 27 BCE, in recognition for his services, Octavian was granted by the Roman Senate the title of 'Augustus'; it is at this point that scholars tend to set the beginning of the Roman 'empire'. But what did it really mean to be 'emperor' at this point? First, the emperor was better known as *princeps*, a 'first among equals' in the Roman nobility; someone who was simply first, but not essentially different from all the others (for convenience, however, in this book we shall use the terms *princeps* and emperor interchangeably). What did distinguish the *princeps* from the other senators was his possession of two specific powers: the *tribunicia potestas* and the *imperium proconsulare maximum*. The former granted whoever possessed it (usually a tribune of the plebs) *sacrosanctitas* – the inviolability of his own person – and the power of veto over any legislation brought forward in the Senate; the latter allowed its owner to exercise executive and judicial authority over all the provinces and the armies outside Italy. Whilst Augustus was still alive, whoever else was granted these two powers could be seen as the potential successor to the first emperor.

Augustus' right hand in the first half of his life was Agrippa, who was at one point wedded to Augustus' only daughter, Julia (the Elder). They had five children, among whom were Gaius Caesar and Lucius Caesar. These two boys were adopted by Augustus as his own sons and heirs even before their father's death in 12 BCE; by so doing, the first emperor intended to train them to succeed him as *principes* after his death. Another child of the couple was Agrippina, the future wife of Germanicus.

Germanicus himself was linked to Augustus via his grandmother, Octavia, Augustus' only sister. His mother, Antonia (Octavia's daughter) was also the daughter of Mark Antony. Therefore, the blood of both the great generals of Actium flowed in the young prince's veins. On his paternal side, Germanicus was descended from one of the oldest and noblest houses of Rome: the Claudii. His father, Drusus the Elder, and his uncle Tiberius were the offspring of one Claudius and Livia Drusilla. Livia had divorced her husband and married Augustus before the end of the civil wars, when Tiberius was already born and whilst Drusus the Elder was still in her belly (a factor which was the cause of much gossip in Rome at the time). Antonian, Julian and Claudian ancestry: Germanicus could claim all three of them and it would have made him the perfect candidate for the imperial throne.

Germanicus' link to the dynasty's founder was further strengthened by his marriage to Augustus' granddaughter, Agrippina. Their children, who included the future emperor Caligula and Agrippina the Younger, mother of Nero, could thus also boast direct descent from Augustus in addition to all their other claims.

Germanicus grew up following the example of his father Drusus the Elder, who had achieved brilliant military victories in Germania (this is why the prince, whose original name was

Claudius Drusus, later came to be known as Germanicus). Drusus the Elder greatly contributed to the expansion of the empire beyond the Rhine river before tragically dying in 9 BCE, from an infected wound following a fall from his horse. Germanicus was also brought up in a household where conjugal love was clearly present; his mother was said to have been much devoted to her husband and, after Drusus the Elder's death, she refused to marry again.

Germanicus had two siblings: a brother, Claudius, and a sister, Livilla. Claudius was always treated as 'defective' by his elders, probably because of a physical imperfection of some kind.[27] He was shunned and kept away from public office as much as possible, but ironically, he later proved himself to be a very competent and skilful emperor. Livilla first married Augustus' grandson and heir, Gaius Caesar; when the young man died prematurely in 4 CE, she was remarried to her uncle Tiberius' only son, Drusus the Younger.[28]

The year 4 CE marked a pivotal step in Germanicus' early life. At the death of his heir Gaius Caesar (Lucius Caesar had died in 2 CE), Augustus was once again in need of finding a suitable candidate to succeed him. The choice fell on Tiberius, who at that point was the most senior and experienced man alive in the household after the patriarch himself. Tiberius was thus formally adopted by Augustus as his own son and heir, together with the patriarch's last remaining grandson, Agrippa Postumus. After conferring on Tiberius both the *tribunicia potestas* and the *imperium proconsulare*, Augustus had his newly adopted son adopt Germanicus in his turn, thus catapulting the young prince to the forefront of the imperial succession. This was in spite of the presence of Tiberius' own son, Drusus the Younger; we shall explore the old patriarch's reasons for such a choice later below (see Chapter 2). For now, what matters is that Augustus clearly had some dynastic plans in mind for this young boy; after all Germanicus was linked to him by blood, unlike Tiberius. Augustus' dynastic intentions are also confirmed by his sanction of the marriage between Germanicus and his granddaughter Agrippina in 4 or 5 CE.

Between 7 and 9 CE, Germanicus saw his first, formal military action. He was appointed as aide to Tiberius in the Illyricum (the modern-day Balkan area) to help him quell a major revolt that had broken out there. It is in relation to this that the first mentions of the young prince's prowess are recorded, such as his defeat of the Mazaei (or Maezaei) tribe and his plunder of the rebel stronghold of Raetinium in Dalmatia.

In 9 CE, when Germanicus was acclaimed *imperator*[29] by the troops for the first time, trouble struck in Germany. Publius Quinctilius Varus' three legions were annihilated by a German coalition of tribes led by Arminius, the chief of the Cherusci. The three legionary military insignia were lost and the defeat put a stop to Augustan expansion beyond the Rhine river, effectively jeopardizing Rome's control of the whole area. Germanicus thus followed his uncle/stepfather Tiberius to Germany, where they campaigned incessantly to salvage the situation. It was also during this period that the prince achieved (much earlier than was normal) the highest post a Roman aristocrat could strive for: the consulship, which he gained in 12 CE.

On the eve of Augustus' death, in 14 CE, Germanicus was in Gaul making preparations for another military campaign beyond the Rhine. Tiberius was already back in Rome after celebrating his triumph in 13 CE (the same triumph in which Velleius Paterculus took part). We will see in Chapter 2 what took place at the news of the old patriarch's death. Before that, however, we take a leap in time and begin with the end – dealing with Germanicus' death first will I hope make clear, reader, the perceptions that contemporaries had of this promising young man and by the same token give you a better understanding of his life.

Chapter 1

10 October 19 CE

1.1 The mysterious death of a beloved man

Their friends were waiting anxiously in the antechamber. Their son and baby daughters had been left with the wet-nurse in an area of the palace far from that stifling atmosphere. From outside, through wide open doors and windows, came the murmuring of the crowd, gathered from far and wide, expecting news. Suddenly, the curtains on the threshold parted and a slender figure emerged from the darkness of the chamber beyond. Everything stopped; all fell silent. You could feel the tension rising up, as if a swarm of flies had suddenly erupted into the overcrowded room. Agrippina stepped forward, the autumnal rays hitting her gaunt face, revealing the pain of the past few weeks. For once Augustus' granddaughter kept her head low, her gaze to the floor, hidden from view. A solitary tear glimmered on her chiselled cheek, trickling down to that chin of such divine form. A moment later, the whole of Antioch burst out in a cry of grief.

* * *

Such could well have been the atmosphere in the capital of the province of Syria on that fateful sixth day before the Ides of October, in the year in which consuls were M. Silanus and L. Norbatus – in modern terms, 10 October 19 CE. All the historical sources that record the event agree on the impact that Germanicus' death had: not only was the Roman populace affected, but even the barbarians beyond the borders of the empire were saddened by his loss.[1] We could with reason define Germanicus' death as an event of ecumenical consequence; or this is at least what the Roman sources want us to believe.

Very interestingly, some modern authors compare the description of this event to the passing of a much more famous young general, who also died prematurely and in mysterious circumstances: Alexander the Great. Historian Lorenzo Braccesi frames this 'universal grief' for Germanicus' death within the heroic frame of the *imitatio Alexandri* – or the imitation of Alexander.[2] It was indeed customary for successful Roman generals to be compared to Alexander the Great for their heroic deeds and military exploits.[3] Alexander was the ultimate figure every proud general would aspire to equal. The most obvious example of this is Julius Caesar, who surged to fame in just eight years due to his glorious conquest of Gaul. But others before him had already boosted their standing by calling attention to the comparison between themselves and the young Macedonian king – men such as Scipio Africanus and Pompey the Great, to name but two. Moreover, many Roman authors themselves indulged in such comparisons, to raise the profile of their parvenu state against the prestige of the Hellenistic kingdoms. Germanicus was just the last in a long list of individuals whose deeds were assimilated with those of the legendary Alexander. Even the premature death of the conqueror of Asia had been received with consternation by his subjects; this is just the first of many comparisons between the two men which we will encounter.

But did Germanicus' sudden passing spark such profound grief in his contemporaries purely because he was regarded as something of a 'new Alexander'? It seems this is not the whole story. The historical sources are dotted with praise for Germanicus, a young man cloaked in virtue and other positive qualities which endeared him greatly to the people and made him one of the most beloved figures of his time. Tacitus describes Germanicus as showing 'humanity towards allies, mildness towards his enemies' and talks of the respect that he generated in anyone who saw and heard him.[4] Suetonius is no less impressed:

> It is the general opinion that Germanicus possessed all the highest qualities of body and mind, to a degree never equalled by anyone; a handsome person of unequalled valour, master of both Greek and Latin eloquence and culture, he attracted the love of men for his peculiar kindness and for a remarkable capacity for winning men's affection. [...] Unassuming at home and abroad, he always entered the free and federate towns without lictors. Wherever he came upon the tombs of distinguished men, he always offered sacrifice to their shades. [...] Even towards his detractors, whosoever they were and whatever their motives, he was mild and lenient [...].'[5]

And Cassius Dio's comment is not dissimilar:

> Germanicus, of handsome body and of highest virtue, also distinguished himself for his education and for his strength; and although he showed bravery in the face of his enemies, he behaved amiably with his peers. Despite his great power as Caesar,[6] he kept his ambition low, like a common man; he was never cruel with his subjects; he was not jealous of Drusus (the Younger) nor did he show reproachful behaviour towards Tiberius. In a word, he was one of those few men who never made a mistake and who did not allow his fate to overtake him.[7]

After such eulogies we can see there was something more to Germanicus than just being a 'new Alexander', at least according to our literary sources. In reading the ancient authors, it is clear how improvements to the Alexandrian model had also been made: to the virtues usually associated with Alexander, such as bravery and cunning, were added some peculiar to Germanicus only – mercy, moderation, and tolerance, to name just three.[8] We are thus in the presence of a new model without the flaws of the original: one wholly 'positive new Alexander'.

We can now more easily understand why the shock which engulfed the empire at hearing of such a man's death was so great. In addition to all the above, the young man had been destined to don the imperial purple after the passing of his uncle Tiberius, the current emperor. Germanicus had indeed been bestowed with the *tribunicia potestas,* one of the two core powers which characterized a Roman emperor (see Introduction). When the Senate – with the agreement of Tiberius – conferred this power on Germanicus along with the *imperium proconsulare* in 18 CE (just before his departure for the eastern provinces), it was just acting upon the late Augustus' will. In 4 CE, when Augustus had formally adopted Tiberius as his son and heir, he had at the same time directed him to adopt Germanicus, though Tiberius already had a biological son, Drusus 'the Younger'.[9] In this way Augustus was asserting the right of Germanicus to succeed his uncle once the time came.

As it happened, however, Drusus' presence was never a problem for Germanicus, nor vice versa the two brothers used to get along perfectly well.[10] Before travelling east, Germanicus visited Drusus in the Illyricum (a region which included many modern Balkan states); and it was Drusus alone who, along with the future emperor Claudius (Germanicus' biological brother), went to meet and escort the ashes of the young general on their way back to Rome;[11] and also Drusus who took care of and protected Germanicus' sons after his passing.[12] Thus the hypothetical issue of a struggle of power between the two young men never materialized, and after few years Drusus followed his brother to the grave, in 23 CE.

We shall now focus on Germanicus' death: undoubtedly a mysterious one and the object of speculation ever since it happened, fascinating to historians and the curious alike for the aura of ambiguity which surrounds it. At the time some believed it was death due to natural causes, but there were many more who suspected murder. Germanicus himself, apparently, believed he had been poisoned.[13] Some sources report that Germanicus' body showed evident signs of poisoning: bruised all over, foaming at the mouth, an intact heart after the body had been burnt (it was believed that a heart full of poison could not be burnt).[14] Who could blame people for believing that something was indeed amiss? Moreover, the coincidences and contrasts of behaviour among the imperial family were so remarkable that it was very difficult to believe that a simple disease had taken away one of the greatest and most beloved men that Rome had ever had – the new Alexander! The actions of Piso, the governor of Syria, and his wife Plancina at the news of Germanicus' illness and subsequent death had been barely orthodox; and what the emperor Tiberius and his mother Livia did – or rather, did not do – at the time of the funeral rites in Rome was little short of blasphemy. There were even rumours that it had been Tiberius himself who had commissioned Piso to dispose of his nephew.[15] But, as we shall see, the facts shed a different light on matters depending on the way we choose to look at them.

Thus far, I have deliberately left out Tacitus' account of events – usually considered our most authoritative source – as he confessed himself (with some regret) to be highly sceptical about what really happened at the time. His narrative differs from the one given by Suetonius and Cassius Dio (who probably used the same source for this particular event). Tacitus states that 'the body [...] was exposed in the Forum of Antioch, the place appointed for the cremation; but whether it exhibited signs of poisoning or not is uncertain.'[16] This passage sounds very different from the certainty with which Cassius Dio confirms the event! In an earlier section, the Roman historian mentions that Germanicus himself was convinced that he had been poisoned by Piso. It is worth reporting the quote in full:

> He then went down to Seleucia to await the issue of the malady, which had come on once more, and was aggravated by a conviction in the mind of Germanicus that he had been poisoned by Piso. Remains of disinterred human bodies had been found beneath the floor and in the walls of the house, together with spells and magical formulae; leaden tablets with the name of Germanicus inscribed upon them; charred and blood-stained human ashes, and other baleful substances by which people believe that souls may be devoted to the Gods below. Piso was also accused of sending messengers to spy out unfavourable symptoms in the case.
>
> This roused the fears, not less than the indignation, of Germanicus. If his threshold were to be beset, if he had to draw his last breath under the eyes of his enemies, what would become of his unhappy wife and his infant children? Poisoning, it would seem, was too slow a process; Piso was in hot haste to be in sole command of the province and the legions. But Germanicus had not yet sunk so low; nor would the murderer reap the recompense of his crime. With that he wrote a letter renouncing Piso's friendship; many add that he ordered him out of the province.
>
> For a moment Germanicus rallied, and hoped to revive; but his strength again failed, and as his end drew nigh, he thus addressed the friends who stood beside him: 'If I were paying my debt to Nature, I might deem that I had a grievance even against the Gods for snatching me thus, so young, and before my time, from my parents, my children and my country. But now that my days have been cut short by the guilty hands of Piso and Plancina, I leave my last prayers with you. Tell my father and my brother what cruel wrongs I have endured, by what artifices I have

been beset: how I have ended a miserable life by a most unhappy death.'[17]

According to this, Germanicus obviously believed that he had been poisoned by Piso and his wife Plancina. The historian's declaration finds confirmation in a bronze inscription which contains the Senate's dispositions over the fate of Piso – a striking document which has been preserved in a copy incised on a bronze slab found in Spain.[18] We will meet Piso again (in Chapter 3) and examine what may have led Germanicus to believe such a thing. We will also try to understand how the dying words of the young man could possibly have been recorded and made known – who could have been in the room to know what Germanicus exactly said? Surely not Tacitus, as he lived roughly a hundred years after the events. Tacitus' source? But who was this source? For now, it is worth repeating that already, among Germanicus' contemporaries, versions of the events differed in whether 'men were inclined towards Germanicus by compassion and preconceived suspicion, or towards Piso by friendship.'[19]

This last sentence of Tacitus' work gives confirmation to the fact that two opposing traditions of the event were included in the *Annals* during its composition: one 'pro-Germanicus' and one 'pro-Piso'.[20] Both versions were embroidered by the respective circle of friends of these two individuals, with aims that went well beyond researching the truth of Germanicus' death. The *factio germaniciana* had a concept of the principate which in turn Caesar, Mark Antony, Julia (daughter of Augustus) and her entourage had adopted: they wanted Rome to become an absolute monarchy on the example of the Hellenistic kingdoms – Egypt prime among them, with its millenarian tradition of divine rulership (see more on this in Chapter 2.3). This would be a monarchy short of divinity, ill-matched with the conservatism of aristocratic Rome. Rather, such traditionalism was embedded in the moderate policy of Augustus, who had achieved the perfect solution by styling his de facto monarchy a 'principality'– that is, he was *princeps* rather than king, 'the first' among the many aristocrats of Rome. Meanwhile, conservatism and respect for the *mos maiorum* (literally 'the way of the ancestors' and the unwritten social code of the Romans) and for the old republican institutions, typical of the most traditionalist wing of the Senate, was a trait of those who formed Piso's circle of friends.

Some modern authors have endorsed Tacitus' scepticism, aware that a definitive solution to the matter may never be reached.[21] Among them the notion prevails that Germanicus may indeed have died of natural causes, in which case it was Germanicus' wife Agrippina who, together with their circle of friends, created the whole poisoning affair in order to implicate, ultimately and indirectly, Tiberius.[22] After all, it had been he who had allegedly given Piso 'secret instructions' before the governor joined Germanicus in Syria.[23] As I will set out in later chapters, the latter line of thought seems the more accurate of the two: that Germanicus effectively passed away due to natural causes, but people close to him then exploited the unexpected situation by creating a 'plot' for their own practical political gains (see Chapters 2.3 and 3).

But what led so many contemporaries to believe that Germanicus had in effect been poisoned, and that it had been at the behest of no one less than his uncle, the emperor? And what did Tiberius stand to gain by disposing of his stepson, his blood relative and heir presumptive? We answer the second question in the next chapter; in order to answer the first, we need to see what happened during Germanicus' funeral and examine the posthumous honours that the Senate (and the emperor) bestowed on him.

1.2 Funerals and honours

Germanicus' body was cremated at Antioch and his ashes were gathered in an urn which his widow carried to Rome, holding it tight to her breast. Tacitus' description of Agrippina's arrival at Brundisium (modern-day Brindisi, in southern Italy) is quite picturesque: it is said that, at the sight of her sorry state, the urn pressed to her bosom, 'with no certainty of vengeance, full of fears for herself, and exposed at so many points to the attacks of fortune by her ill-starred fertility, all hearts were filled with compassion.'[24] The highest honours were paid to Germanicus by towns on the way back to Rome and at Terracina (in southern Latium), the funeral procession was met by Drusus the Younger, Claudius (the future emperor), Germanicus' two eldest sons (Nero and Drusus Caesar, who had remained in Rome while their parents were abroad), the Senate, the two consuls for the new year (20 CE) and a 'large part of the populace'.[25] From Terracina, this human river carried on, making its way to the capital.

* * *

Sunlight was quickly warming up the mild winter's day. The marble decorations of the temples and the basilicas were gleaming, conferring a sacred aura to the event, as if the vaulted sky itself had come down to earth to claim that extraordinary man. The crowd was waiting with trepidation; it couldn't be much longer now. Now, voices began to rise steadily from the southern side of the forum, the hush transforming into cries of grief intermittent and broken; and then came the procession, appearing from behind the Temple of the Divus Julius and down the Sacred Way. The luckiest ones, those who had spent the icy night on the hard stone slabs, were now compensated for their suffering: a golden urn shone radiantly between the hands of Agrippina, as if to distract that tired and distraught figure, clad in a grey cloak that hid her beauty. Then came her sons, auburn-haired, young promises of the empire; soon the love that the people had had for their father would be bestowed upon their heads; but this was not the day to praise their virtues and their future success. Here was Drusus then, along with Claudius, followed closely by the two consuls, and the senators and... but wait–

where was Tiberius Caesar? And the Augusta? And Antonia, the young prodigy's own mother? How could a mother not be present at such an event? And something else was missing: where was the pomp necessary to the rank and prestige of such a man, the images of the ancestors, an unmissable element of any Roman funeral worthy of the name? They wondered too, why was the procession not stopping there, in the forum, where the 'laudatio' was always pronounced in such circumstances? A whisper was quickly hushed somewhere among the stunned crowd: the emperor was not present as he was currently busy with feasting and drinking at home.

* * *

Tacitus informs us that Tiberius and his mother Livia did not attend the funeral because they believed that grieving publicly was not appropriate to their rank, or 'perhaps because they feared that, if exposed to the public gaze, their faces might betray their insincerity.' Antonia, moreover, is said to have been prevented by the imperial couple from joining the procession as they wanted people to see that they were grieving in the same way as the young man's own mother.[26]

Let us begin with this final matter, the alleged order from Tiberius and Livia that Antonia stay home. The cordial relations that Antonia and Tiberius maintained throughout their life hardly tallies with Tacitus' account.[27] Moreover, it was Antonia who convinced Tiberius, later on in the reign, of the danger that Sejanus, the emperor's praetorian prefect, represented; something she would surely not have done had she truly resented her brother-in-law.[28] Tiberius' quick reaction in the disposal of his omnipresent adviser shows the trust that he put in the advice and opinion of his sister-in-law. If there was still that trust in 31 CE, the year of Sejanus' fall, it is unlikely that it was any less at the time of Germanicus' death. It is more probable that Antonia herself decided not to attend her son's funeral, wishing to present a united front with Tiberius and the matriarch Livia. It is also interesting to note that Antonia emerged as a public figure only after Livia's death in 29 CE, replacing her as 'first lady' of the empire.

Now we can turn to the reason why Tiberius did not attend his nephew's funeral. To modern feelings this may seem shocking. Some authors argue that Tiberius did not want to compete with Agrippina's popularity among the people of Rome, hence his (and his mother's) absence from the obsequies.[29] However, the 'coldness' which the sources attribute to Tiberius on many occasions was actually part of his own vision of his role in the state, rather than an aspect of character. It was his view that private matters must not in any way interfere with the ordinary, day-to-day running of government. No exceptions could be made; the state could not wait. Indeed, it was not only for Germanicus that Tiberius made no exception – we know that he kept attending Senate sessions throughout the final illness of his biological son Drusus, and continued 'even after he [Drusus] had died but had not yet been buried'.[30] Even Cassius Dio noticed that, although Tiberius was very attached to his son, 'such was the behaviour that he maintained on every occasion'.[31] Similarly, when one of his grandchildren passed away unexpectedly, the old emperor did not interrupt public activities: 'he did not think it right in any case that one who was governing others should neglect his care of the public interest because of his private misfortunes, and moreover he was trying to accustom others not to jeopardize the interests of the living on account of the dead.'[32] When his mother died, he did not attend her obsequies either.[33] Nor were joyous events treated any differently: he did not attend the weddings of two of Germanicus' daughters and even the Senate kept convening and deliberating on judicial cases as usual.[34]

So many examples should be proof enough that, rather than not attending because he was at home secretly drinking and enjoying himself, Tiberius did not preside at Germanicus' funeral due to a simple sense of decorum (cold-hearted though this can appear to us today). It was all part of a sense of decency inherent in Tiberius' conservative character and vision of the state. He was very conscious of his aristocratic and republican heritage (his family, the *gens Claudia*, was one of the oldest and most illustrious of the old Republic) and believed he could not be seen to put private affairs before matters of state. Duty first, no matter the personal cost. That contemporary Roman aristocracy were in tune with these feelings is shown by the praise they showered on Tiberius and Livia for having taught their progeny not to grieve beyond commendable limits.[35]

Despite such beliefs, in our sources we do read of Tiberius attending the obsequies of prominent citizens and honouring many of them with public funerals.[36] How can we thus reconcile these two apparently contrasting behaviours? To answer this question we need to bear in mind an important point which will resurface again and again in our story, and from which many later misinterpretations stemmed: the blurring of public and private domains. The imperial family was meant to reflect the higher status that the first emperor, Augustus, had among the aristocracy: a simple *primus inter pares*, or first among equals. In consequence, his household became the most prominent family in Rome, the family of the capital's first citizen. Their names, however, did not yet appear in public acts, nor were its members (especially the women) any different from other nobility. During the later years of Augustus' principate and the beginning of Tiberius' reign, the imperial family began an internal transformation that saw them shifting from the private sphere to the public stage. Its members were not simply private individuals anymore; what happened within the household started to become the concern of many, later becoming entangled with matters of state too.[37]

A concrete instance of this change of attitude towards and perception of the imperial family can be found in a versified letter that the poet Ovid wrote when in exile, after 8 CE. In a public address to Rome, the writer mentions all the prominent members of the *Domus Augusta* alive at that time – not only

Tiberius and Livia, but also Germanicus, Drusus the Younger, Agrippina, Claudia Livilla and Germanicus' two eldest sons.[38] In another letter from the same collection, Ovid recorded the possession of an altar where, beside statues of his own family protectors, were statuettes of members of the imperial family.[39] Images of Germanicus and Drusus flanked those of the old emperor and his mother. Although Ovid may have written this in the hope of being recalled to Rome from his exile, his words should not be discarded as simple flattery; it is clear that the perception of the imperial household in people's minds was changing. For an author like Tacitus, living at a time when what an emperor and his family could or could not do was well established, some of the behaviours of the early *principes* must have appeared shocking. From this state of affairs stems the later authors' usual condemnation or mischaracterization of these rulers' actions and intentions. If Tiberius' behaviour is contextualized within this frame, then it becomes much more coherent and understandable than at first glance. Whereas the emperor considered any family-related matter (such as his own heir's funeral) as a private matter, anything related to other Roman noblemen outside his own house was a public matter and, in consequence, required his presence. It is only by understanding the fluidity between private and public spheres at this stage that events and behaviours which at first seem contradictory begin to make sense.

In Tacitus' narration, the people are said to complain about the modesty of the whole funeral procession, *sine imagine et pompa* (literally 'without imagery and pomp') – and without the fast typical of aristocratic obsequies. Historian Augusto Fraschetti has convincingly explained the reason behind this: as Germanicus' body had already been cremated in Antioch, the measures usually adopted for an 'ordinary' funeral in Rome could thus not be undertaken.[40] In the capital city only the last part of the funerary rite, the ritual deposition of the bones into the tomb (the Mausoleum of Augustus, in this case), took place. Tacitus compares Germanicus' bland funeral to the grandiosity of the one Augustus had organized for his stepson Drusus the Elder, Germanicus' father.[41] The author stresses the comparison in order to disparage Tiberius and to reinforce his thesis that the emperor did not care for Germanicus. However, in the case of Drusus the Elder's funeral, Tiberius himself had gone to Germany to retrieve his body, which was duly cremated in Rome rather than somewhere else, as had happened to Germanicus. The difference thus lies in the adherence to and respect of ritual norms which perfectly agree with Tiberius' conservative character – a trait of his which we have already mentioned.

Tacitus renews his attack on Tiberius when he mentions an edict of the emperor's which put an end to public mourning for the young prince, exhorting citizens to go back to their daily occupations and their amusements.[42] The historian states that public mourning went on until the end of March 20 CE, but Augusto Fraschetti reckons that Suetonius' account is more accurate than Tacitus' in this case. According to the biographer, public mourning continued throughout December (considering that the news of Germanicus' death probably arrived in Rome around the beginning of the month);[43] what Tacitus refers to is not the official mourning period, but the spontaneous attitude of ordinary citizens, whose mourning could well have extended into March. Tiberius' edict would thus have had the effect of restoring the regular daily life of the city once again, months having passed since the placing of the young man's ashes in the Mausoleum of Augustus – the moment at which, ritually and officially, funerals and public mourning ended.

Interestingly, we possess some documentation on the posthumous honours attributed to Germanicus by the Senate. What we can see from these is how the young prince's memory began to be exploited by his stepfather/uncle just months after his death (the ways in which Germanicus' memory was used by other family members will be explored in Chapter 4). Tacitus, who included some of these documents in his history, dedicates a whole passage to the honours and tribute paid to the prince:

> Honours for Germanicus were proposed and decreed by anyone who had reason enough and love for him: it was decided that his name was to be sung in the Carmina Saliaria; that curule chairs (dedicated to him) were to be placed in seats reserved for the *sodales Augustales* (priests of the deified Augustus) and that wreaths of oak leaves were to be placed upon them. It was decreed that an ivory image of Germanicus must precede any procession during chariot races; and that any priest or augur who was meant to replace him had to belong to the *gens Iulia*. Three arches – one in Rome, one on the Rhine bank and the third on Mount Amanus in Syria – were to be dedicated to his memory, bearing an inscription recounting his achievements and his death.[44] In Antioch, where he was cremated, a burial mound was built, also a cenotaph at Epidaphne, where he had passed away. It would be difficult to list all the statues dedicated to him and the places where he was worshipped. It was proposed to dedicate to him a golden shield of considerable size to be put among those of the great orators; but Tiberius declared that he would choose just an ordinary one, identical to all the others, since eloquence could not be judged by one's birth and it would have been enough for Germanicus just to be included among the great Roman writers.[45] The equestrian order decreed that an area of the theatre which had previously been known as 'of the youths' be renamed 'Germanicus' and established that troops followed images of him during the procession on the Ides of July. The majority of these honours lasted a long time; some were immediately abandoned, whereas others were not dropped until later.[46]

We are fortunate enough to have two extraordinary documents which allow us to compare Tacitus' words: the *Tabula Hebana* and the *Tabula Siarensis*, two bronze inscriptions made at the time of the events. The *Tabula Hebana* (see figure 12) consists of two fragments found at Magliano in Tuscany (ancient Heba in Etruria) in 1947, while the *Tabula Siarensis* (from the ancient town of Siarum) was discovered, again in two fragments, in Andalusia in 1982. The two inscriptions (which are incomplete in the form they have been found) record a series of honours dedicated by the Senate to Germanicus after his death, many of which are not present in Tacitus' narrative. For this reason, some scholars believe that the account of the Roman historian might have been based on a third *senatus consultum* (Senate's deposition) whose text coincides only partially with the content of the two tablets.[47]

The *Tabula Hebana* reports the text of the *Rogatio Valeria Aurelia*, a law passed in 5 CE by the Senate (with Augustus' approval) which dealt with the posthumous honours to be awarded to Augustus' late heirs, Gaius Caesar and Lucius Caesar. The honours to Germanicus were added to these, during a Senate session in December 19 CE. Among the tributes not mentioned in Tacitus' account is the creation of five new centuries (that is, groups of Roman citizens ranked by wealth) named after the prince, to be added to the ten already dedicated to Gaius and Lucius. As the two brothers had been Augustus' heirs and were treated as such, in turn, Germanicus was formally presented to the public as Tiberius' heir, in the will of both Senate and emperor (it should be remembered that without Tiberius' approval the law would not have been passed). An *imago clipeata* (portrait on a round shield – the shield mentioned by Tacitus) is named in the text of the *Tabula Hebana*, with no indication of it being golden, however. On the other hand, the *Tabula*'s shield may easily have borne a different image, since it is said to have been erected at the

Senate's meeting place in the portico of the temple of Palatine Apollo, along with the one dedicated to Germanicus' father, Drusus the Elder.[48] This temple had been built by Augustus just next to his private home on the Palatine Hill, and it was a place deeply connected to his dynastic policy.

The fact that such images were located in a public place which was entwined so closely with Augustus' political propaganda – and where even the Senate used to meet – shows again that in those years the boundary between private and public began to merge, sometimes causing misunderstandings.[49] Finally, on each anniversary of Germanicus' death, all temples within a mile of Rome had to be closed and rituals to his *manes* (a difficult concept, at times translated as 'souls' or 'spirits') had to be offered. While analysing this text, historian Wolfgang Lebek made a distinction which is worth mentioning: honours can be classified as pertaining to 'memory' or to 'mourning'. Tributes aiming to 'keep the deceased alive' by having him take part in public functions – such as the creation of the five centuries or the dedication of curule chairs – belong to the first category. Related to 'mourning' are all those honours which acknowledge an individual's death and which demonstrate the grief of those still alive.[50]

The *Tabula Siarensis* reports the text of a different senatorial decree: the *senatus consultum de honoribus Germanici decernendis* (decision of the Senate regarding honours for Germanicus). No fewer than twenty-seven honours are recorded in the extant parts of the tablet – a great contrast with the few listed by Tacitus. The Senate is said to have consulted the whole imperial family – women included (something unprecedented) – on the tributes to be paid to Germanicus. This tablet also gives a better description of the triumphal arch that the Senate dedicated to Germanicus' memory in Rome: it was erected in the Circus Flaminius, a public area next to the river Tiber linked with triumphs (Germanicus' own in 17 CE had passed through here). The area already showcased some dynastic buildings which Augustus had built in memory of members of his family: the Theatre of Marcellus, dedicated to his first heir, precociously deceased, and the Porticus of Octavia, named in honour of his only sister and the mother of Marcellus (and Germanicus' own grandmother). The choice of such a place – approved by Tiberius – is key to understanding the position that the young man had in the imperial household: if the emperor had been so jealous and fearful of his stepson/nephew, surely he would not have allowed a triumphal arch in his memory to be erected in such a central location! The inscription on the arch commemorated Germanicus' death 'for the sake of the *res publica*' and statues of Germanicus' nuclear family (biological father, mother, brother, wife and older children) were placed on top of it beside his own. Interestingly, there is no mention of a statue to Tiberius here, as this monument was a personal commemoration for the private memory of the young man, not a political statement of the likes of the sculptural group found in Palmyra (see below, Chapter 4.1). The fact that statues of the family's women and children were present on a type of monument which would usually display only military decorations and inscriptions is another testimony to the changing nature of the imperial family, from private household to public entity.[51]

We have already mentioned Tiberius' conservative outlook and choices in public. Why would such a traditional ruler allow the Senate to dedicate a triumphal arch displaying something so unprecedented as statues of family members, including women and children? Let us remember that, as holder of the tribunician power, the emperor could veto any proposal of the Senate he deemed inappropriate. Why would he have allowed Germanicus' children, including his daughters, to ride on their father's chariot during his triumph of 17 CE? In stressing the place that Germanicus occupied within the imperial household (and notwithstanding all the rumours regarding his death), did Tiberius think that, in so doing, he could strengthen the position of the family in the public eye?

The answer to such questions may lie in the *Tabula Siarensis*. The Senate is said to have voted such honours 'so that the more easily the *pietas* of all orders towards the *Domus Augusta* and the consensus of all citizens to honour the memory of Germanicus Caesar might be apparent.'[52] Historian Beth Severy convincingly argues that the word *pietas*, a term usually translated as 'respect', at that time meant something more akin to 'affection/emotion'.[53] Tiberius thus allowed the Senate and the people to show their affection for Germanicus by paying him such honours. The emperor could have been jealous of his nephew, but surely it was good politics to keep his citizens happy by allowing them to express their feelings. However, that he himself may have partaken of such emotions emerges from another passage of the *Tabula Siarensis*, 'so that the pietas of Drusus Caesar [in this case, Drusus the Younger] may be better attested, it is pleasing that the pamphlet, which he recited at the recent meeting of the Senate, be inscribed in bronze with the senatorial decree that was passed.'[54] We know that Drusus the Younger was present at Germanicus' funeral, but not Tiberius – for propriety, the emperor had not shown himself, but had allowed the younger generation to represent the imperial household. Might Tiberius not have done the same sort of thing with the 'pamphlet' mentioned in the *Tabula Siarensis* – that is, by having Drusus as his representative at the Senate meeting? In that case the *pietas* of Drusus would come to embody, beyond his own, the affection that Tiberius felt for his recently departed nephew and heir presumptive.

Tacitus makes no mention of the imperial family being consulted by the Senate to discuss what was proper to pay tribute to Germanicus, in contrast with the *Tabula Siarensis*. Some scholars believe that the historian consciously omitted the fact that the Senate had conferred with the family, as this would not agree with the atmosphere of his narrative. According to this view, Tacitus would have deliberately left out information that could tell against the type of characters he was developing – a cold and heartless emperor, in this case.[55] If this is really the case, on how many other occasions might Tacitus have twisted his account to fit the purposes of his narrative? Could other authors have done the same? To what extent did the often quoted fear and jealousy of Tiberius towards Germanicus correspond to truth? The next chapter will try to answer these questions.

Chapter 2

A 'Constructed' Hatred?

Earlier we wondered why, according to the *rumores*, Tiberius might have ended up with having his nephew and heir eliminated – Germanicus must have been a very troublesome individual if the emperor dared to act so ruthlessly. But does this hatred that Tiberius allegedly had for his stepson represent the real picture? How close to the truth is it that the emperor feared he might be dethroned by this popular and charismatic young man? Or was the quarrelsome relationship between uncle and nephew mere construction – or sometimes 'created' out of nowhere – by our historical sources? And if so, why would they do this?

This chapter will explore the possible answers to these questions in retracing some of the most salient moments of Germanicus' life, especially the points at which the supposed conflict between him and Tiberius was most acute. We first examine Germanicus' activity on the Rhine frontier and in Germany in the years 14–16 CE; and then, his mission to the eastern provinces of the empire in 17–18 CE, alongside his visit to Egypt. The final section of the chapter will look at Germanicus' wife Agrippina and the role that she may have had in fostering and creating the myth of the emperor's 'hatred' and jealousy towards her husband.

2.1 On the Rhine and beyond

The first mention of any friction between uncle and nephew in our sources takes place in Germany, along the river Rhine, just after the death of Augustus in 14 CE. Germanicus was at the time in charge of the eight legions garrisoned along the whole length of the river by disposition of the recently deceased emperor, who had also entrusted his young grandson with the administration of Gaul.[1] At the news of Tiberius' succession to Augustus, the four legions under the command of Aulus Caecina (I Germanica, V Alaudae, XX Valeria Victrix and XXI Rapax) rebelled, imitating their comrades stationed in Pannonia (modern-day eastern Austria and Hungary). In contrast with them, however, the Rhine legions did something even more audacious: they acclaimed Germanicus as their new emperor. According to our sources, the legionaries did not want to acknowledge an *imperator* they had not chosen and, since they believed that Germanicus was stronger and more resolute than Tiberius, they decided to throw their lot in with him. In his typically manipulative style, which foreshadows the setting up of a future conflict, Tacitus adds that the soldiers hoped Germanicus would accept their proposal, as they believed that 'he could not tolerate the sovereignty of another.'[2]

Some modern historians believe that our three main sources for these events – Cassius Dio, Suetonius and Tacitus – all referred to one common source, which many locate in the (no longer extant) work of one Servilius Nonianus, who at the time was one of Germanicus' lieutenants.[3] Probably thanks to this common source, we have received a rather homogenous account of the German legions' mutiny, and a consistent view of the behaviour of both Germanicus and Tiberius. Whilst the young general remained loyal to his uncle throughout the rebellion, the emperor is portrayed as fearful of losing his newly acquired position, uncertain of what Germanicus might attempt and jealous of his nephew's popularity with the soldiers. Under more careful analysis, however, Tiberius' so-called *timor* (fear) hardly matches his deeds.

Tacitus informs us that the emperor 'requested the *imperium proconsulare* for Germanicus Caesar' (meaning he asked the Senate); not only did this power allow the young prince to freely administer the provinces assigned to him (Gaul and Germany, in this case), it also permitted him to control the legions located in such provinces.[4] At that time, the eight legions in Germany constituted the mightiest and most numerous section of the imperial army, and whoever was in charge of them had to be someone trustworthy. If Tiberius had not trusted his nephew, surely he would have changed Augustus' dispositions at once – no one whose loyalty was in question would have been allowed to wield such power. Yet Germanicus remained in charge of both the legions and the provinces and repaid his uncle's trust by staying loyal to him.[5]

Tacitus tells us Tiberius was afraid that Germanicus, 'backed by so many legions, the vast reserves of the provinces and a wonderful popularity with the nation, would want to grasp the throne straight away rather than wait for it.'[6] Other passages, however, clash with such a claim, especially when it comes to the popularity Germanicus was said to have enjoyed among his soldiers. Let's go back to Tacitus' narrative once again. When Germanicus finally reached the Rhine after his tour in Gaul (cut short by the mutiny), he immediately addressed the rioting soldiers, imploring them to desist. The legionaries, however, continued trying to give him their support to snatch the throne away from his uncle's hands; and when the young general tried to leave, the soldiers 'barred his way with their weapons, threatening to use them unless he returned.' Germanicus then proposed to commit suicide and grasped the sword of one of the legionaries who, very strangely for men said to be in awe of him, 'urged him to strike himself; while a soldier by the name of Calusidius drew his own blade and offered it [to Germanicus], adding that it was sharper.'[7]

Later on, after the arrival of a senatorial delegation despatched to confer the *imperium proconsulare* on Germanicus, the mutineers, late at night, 'began to shout for the banner [that is, the legionary eagles] in Germanicus' quarters; they forced the door open and, dragging the prince from his bed, they compelled him to hand over the banner under pain of death.'[8] There was also an incident when the soldiers tried to prevent Agrippina and her baby son Gaius (the future Caligula) from leaving the camp – Germanicus, 'still full of grief and indignation', was criticized by everyone 'at that fearful moment' for not taking prompt action.[9] Finally, after the most seditious amongst the rioters were murdered by their own comrades, the young prince, 'among many tears, called that scene not a remedy, but a calamity.'[10]

The tone and details of this narrative should be proof positive that such a commander cannot be considered loved by soldiers who dare to treat him in such a disrespectful manner. Yet if this were the case, why would these hardened legionaries ask a man they did not even respect to become their new emperor? What would they gain by it? At the centre of it all is of course the 'god of money', Mammon, inevitably accompanied by human greed. To better understand the soldiers' choice we need to consider the timing of the mutiny: the legions on the Rhine and in Pannonia rebelled just after Augustus' death, at a very delicate moment for the history of the principate. This was the first time that a new emperor had accessed the throne after the death of a predecessor, and the protocol was definitely unclear – in fact it was not even established. The legionaries were well aware of the power they held: it was thanks to the army's support that Augustus had been able to strengthen his position as the first citizen of Rome over the old aristocracy.[11]

Upon the death of Augustus in 14 CE the mutineers had tried to exploit the precariousness of the situation to attain economic benefits for themselves – more substantial benefits than the emperor had disposed for them in his will. Here is the reason why they were so insistent that Germanicus bid for the imperial purple: if he were to become the new *princeps*, he would surely reward those who had supported him. The soldiers thus hoped to obtain better pay and retirement conditions in gratitude for their help. However, Germanicus disappointed them, stressing his loyalty to his uncle over and over again.[12]

To hammer home his point, the young prince allegedly told the mutineers that even his wife and children did not matter more to him than his father (Tiberius, in this case) and the state.[13] Therefore, from hero, Germanicus became almost a hostage to his own subjects, the same people who were said to revere him; and the danger was so great that at one point the prince was forced to write a letter in Tiberius' name, in which he accepted all the mutineers' demands.[14] That Germanicus was a decisive individual, however, can be seen from the fact that he paid the soldiers' demands out of his own pocket, rather than wait for his uncle's answer. And Tiberius later approved his nephew's decision without complaint, indicating that there was no discord between the two men at this time.

Once the riot was quelled, 'the temper of the soldiers became savage and a sudden desire came over them to advance against the enemy as a means of expiation for their previous madness.'[15] Germanicus appeased his legionaries by organizing a raid in the territory of the Marsi, a Germanic tribe dwelling in woods just beyond the Rhine. During this expedition, a place sacred to the natives, the sanctuary of Tanfana, was destroyed – an act which had a profound psychological effect on the Romans' enemies. Tacitus states that Tiberius 'was then happy that the rising had been crushed [...], but he was also worried about Germanicus' military glory.'[16] Germanicus' glory was destined to increase still more in the following year; so what happened to Tiberius' disquiet? What are the grounds upon which Tacitus made such a claim?

* * *

A dense fog hung upon the trees, so much so that you could scarcely see the tops. It seemed that summer did not exist in these damned lands; while Romans were sweltering at this time of year, the humidity chilled to the bone those so unfortunate as to be here. Germanicus' neck was stiff from the clammy chill and from the weight of his cuirass; he had decided to accompany his men on foot, though he was slightly regretting it right now. 'We are getting close, commander,' whispered Aulus in his ear, 'look.' A fresh chill went through Germanicus, very different from the ones caused by the fog. Nailed to the gnarled trunk of a majestic oak tree was a white skull still wearing its helmet, now rusty, the crest reduced to a few pathetic, discoloured straws, but clearly Roman. Unnerved shouting began as the soldiers spotted more and more of such disconcerting sights, at first so hard to see in their surroundings, as if nature had made them a natural part of herself.

'We should not remain here long; this place is cursed,' ranted Publius somewhere behind Germanicus' shoulders. Although what his legate was saying would have made perfect sense to any rational mind, the young prince could not bring himself to just walk away.

'We have to bury them – all of them,' he whispered. Something within him was insistent; he knew it was the right thing to do, though probably not the wisest. 'We have to bury them!', he repeated loudly, so that all around could hear him clearly. 'Soldiers, these were your brothers; they fought the enemy, they gave their life to Rome, and Rome should not abandon them without remembering their sacrifice, without the proper funerary rites. It's the least they deserve.'

A feeble buzz of agreement went round the troops. But the soldiers who were closest to the generals loudly repeated Germanicus' words, which reverberated down the lines and won him loud cheers – truly this man was one of them.

The advance party now reached the clearing where Varus' last stand had taken place. The remains of the palisades encircling the last camp were still visible here and there among the tall grass. The field was dotted throughout with speckles of white, sad remains of those who had fought until their last breath. It took the soldiers half a day to recover all that they could for burial. Germanicus was the first to throw earth over what was left of the three unfortunate legions. The act warmed the heart of his legionaries and increased their esteem for the young general.

* * *

During the campaign of 15 CE, prepared with great care, one of the three eagles lost by Varus at Teutoburg in 9 AD was discovered (the second one was found the year after, but the third was not found until 41 CE, during Claudius' reign).[17] At the site of the notorious Roman defeat by Arminius, Germanicus was suddenly taken by 'the wish to pay tribute to the (fallen) soldiers and to their commander.'[18] This episode provided new material for all those who took part in building up the prince's *imitatio Alexandri*: the young man is indeed here portrayed as the avenger of Teutoburg.[19] In the clearing where Varus' last camp had stood, Germanicus erected a funerary mound to the fallen soldiers of 9 CE. Interestingly, Tiberius is said to have disapproved of this action and Tacitus is probably right when he claims that the emperor believed that 'a commander, by being an augur and invested with the most ancient priestly honours, should not have presided over funerary rites.'[20] In Rome, anyone who administered sacred rites had to stay away from anything considered 'ritually polluted' – death and funerals were included in this category. We should not forget the great respect that Tiberius had for traditional Roman customs; the fact that he may not have agreed with Germanicus' decision to erect a funerary monument at Teutoburg is thus plausible, although it does not necessarily mean that there was any serious rift between the two men because of this.

According to our sources, however, Tiberius' envy of his nephew's popularity after he found one of the lost eagles and the erection of the commemorative mound at Teutoburg were the main reasons for which the emperor decided to call Germanicus back to Rome. The young prince was acclaimed *imperator* by his own troops and Tiberius awarded his nephew a triumph (a celebratory ritual to commemorate a commander's military achievements).[21] Nonetheless, the military campaign went on for a further year. Are we to believe that Germanicus had rebelled against his uncle's directives?

Matters are more complex than this. Historian Bruno Gallotta has explained how the triumph, in legal terms, signalled the end of Germanicus' *imperium proconsulare* and his augurate.[22] Since the legions had not achieved satisfactory results, Tiberius claimed the right to take decisions back to himself and away from Germanicus, perhaps in order to implement a more effective strategy. It doesn't, however, mean that Tiberius had the intention to terminate hostilities, and the campaign of 16 CE is the confirmation of that. Moreover, we should not ignore that Spain and Italy were named among the provinces which provided supplies to Germanicus' legions for this campaign. The young prince had authority solely over Gaul; the mention of two additional provinces is an indication that such help originating from other parts of the empire could not have come without the emperor's approval.

In 16 CE, a new campaign into Germanic territory was thus launched. This time, Germanicus decided to split his army: one part would thrust into Germany overland, while he himself commanded a fleet that would sail down the Rhine into the North Sea, proceed eastwards and thence upstream on the river Weser.[23] There are some scholars who believe that the narrative of Germanicus' sea journey has been modelled on the account of Alexander the Great's voyage down the Indus river and into the Indian Ocean; according to them, this 'moulding' should be read as another attempt by the ancient sources (probably by some members of Germanicus' 'party') to create an ideological link between the two young generals – so another element of Germanicus' *imitatio Alexandri.*[24]

In imitation of Alexander or not, Germanicus did indeed sail up the river Weser, advancing as far as Idistavisus, an unidentified location which Tacitus tells us was a plain 'lying between the Weser and some [wooded] hills'.[25] Here the Roman legions met the enemy. The German tribesmen, still led by Arminius, launched themselves down the slopes and Germanicus ordered the cavalry to encircle them from the sides. At that moment, eight eagles were spotted flying towards the wooded slopes. Interpreting this as a sign of divine benevolence, Germanicus ordered his men to advance; the move created chaos and panic among the German warriors who, according to Tacitus, began running in two groups towards each other: the tribesmen on the plain retreated towards the hill, whereas the soldiers on the slopes, unaware of their comrades' attempt to flee, kept rushing downwards. Arminius, who had been previously wounded, succeeded in escaping the massacre; but the majority of those who tried fleeing by the river were either shot or dragged away by the force of the current.[26] After the defeat, the Germans regrouped in a valley which the Angrivarii tribe had fortified with an earthwork; the Romans, however, followed suit. Once the earthwork was taken with the help of 'war machines' (probably large scorpions, by their description), Germanicus launched himself into the woods at the rear, at the head of his praetorians. The legions had scored another victory and after this they began their homebound journey.[27]

At this point, the literary accounts state that Germanicus was at odds with Tiberius because the emperor had decided to terminate the campaign earlier than his nephew would have liked and had recalled him to Rome. But the young prince was not at loggerheads with his stepfather, as is testified by the words upon the military trophy which he erected to commemorate the great victory at Idistavisus. Tacitus reports the wording: 'After subduing the peoples between the Rhine and the Elbe rivers, the army of Tiberius Caesar consecrated these memorials to Mars, Jupiter and Augustus.'[28] The young prince makes no mention of his own name – something he could easily have done, had he been in the mood to challenge his uncle and defy his order to come back. Yet we are told that Tiberius recalled his nephew out of envy and hatred, as 'for hatred he [Tiberius] wanted to strip Germanicus of that honour that he had gained.'[29] Was this really the case?

To better understand why Tiberius did not allow Germanicus to continue campaigning beyond the Rhine we need to go back and analyse the background of the emperor himself. Tiberius had led armies in Germany several times, from just after his brother Drusus' death in 9 BCE up to 10–12 CE, long after Varus' defeat at Teutoburg.[30] Interestingly, Tiberius is said, especially after 9 CE, to have waged war upon the enemy aggressively 'when his father [Augustus] and his country would have been content to let him hold them in check.'[31] Does not Augustus' attitude towards Tiberius resemble what Tiberius himself did with Germanicus? Furthermore, Tiberius is said to have 'completed his difficult task in Gaul' in 10 CE, mirroring exactly Germanicus' position there in 13–14 CE. This probably refers to the preparations for an offensive campaign beyond the Rhine, as in the case of his nephew/stepson.[32] And again, similar to what Tiberius did for Germanicus in 17 CE, Augustus had conferred a triumph upon his adopted son and heir after he came back from Germany in 12 CE.[33] All these are more than simple anecdote; they are proof that Germanicus' position as heir to Tiberius was quite self-evident and guaranteed. The young prince was simply taking the same steps that Tiberius himself had taken under Augustus, when he had been the first emperor's heir apparent.

The combination of these two factors – Tiberius' wide experience and knowledge of Germany and the similarity between Germanicus' position and his stepfather's at that particular stage of life – shows that jealousy was not the emperor's motive in recalling Germanicus to Rome after Idistavisus. Tiberius' personal experience had given him the occasion to study the enemy at close quarters and devise a suitable strategy to tackle them, since he was also a capable general. All the efforts that his brother Drusus the Elder had made to subdue the area between the Rhine and the Elbe rivers had been nullified by the defeat at Teutoburg; the majority of the tribes in this area were hostile to Rome and the woodlands were an inhospitable terrain, economically weak and difficult to control. Even the development of any kind of infrastructure there would have been hard, never mind the cost. Tiberius allowed his nephew to avenge Varus' lost legions and to secure the borders with Gaul; once this was achieved with the battle of Idistavisus, Rome's glory was mended and a new phase could begin.[34]

The Rhine frontier had been secured; diplomacy could now replace active warfare. Tiberius was no neophyte in this: he had already dealt with the Suebian kingdom of Maroboduus and its surrounding tribes in just such a way.[35] The aim was precise: to weaken the Germanic tribes by pitting them against each other, thus preventing them from coalescing and posing a concrete threat to Rome. True, the idea of conquest was probably never completely abandoned – as Tiberius' alleged words to Germanicus show. (According to Tacitus, Tiberius induced Germanicus to return 'in order to leave occasion for glory to his brother Drusus [the Younger] too.')[36] Nevertheless, the emperor's longsightedness was well rewarded: following Germanicus' campaigns the German frontier remained quiet and stable for at least two centuries, save only occasional minor disturbances. And if there was ever a divergence between the emperor and his heir, we may describe it in the words of historian Bruno Gallotta, as 'a tactical disagreement within an agreement of strategy'.[37] Whereas for Tiberius the campaign ended with the victory at Idistavisus, Germanicus may have considered it concluded only after the defeat of the Cherusci and the capture of Arminius – though this is something we cannot be certain of.

Whatever the answer however, the main reason Tiberius called Germanicus back to Rome had nothing to do with petty feelings; it was a matter of shrewd politics, as we shall see next.

2.2 Travelling eastwards: in the land of the pharaohs

While Germanicus was busy chasing Arminius through the German forests, trouble was brewing in the east. The Parthians – Rome's single major enemy on the eastern frontier – rejected their philo-Roman king Vonones for one Artabanus, who had been brought up following 'the ancestral manners'. Vonones fled to nearby Armenia, a neutral buffer state between the two superpowers of Parthia and Rome, and eventually became its king. Due to his background and political stance, this development risked upsetting the geopolitical balance of the region, with Artabanus open to the concept of invasion of the Roman-controlled areas. In order to prevent this, the then Roman governor of Syria, Creticus Silanus, summoned Vonones to Antioch and made him a virtual hostage.[38] In such a delicate situation, Tiberius needed someone experienced and reliable in the area to oversee matters so as to prevent further escalation; and who better than his stepson and heir Germanicus, who had just given him proof of his talents and his loyalty?

The tradition of sending the emperor's prospective heir to oversee the eastern regions was not new; precedents had already been set up under Augustus. Agrippa, Augustus' junior colleague in the empire as holder of both *tribunicia potestas* and *imperium proconsulare*, had travelled eastwards between 17 and 13 BCE; his authority extended 'over all those governors of the provinces to the east of the Ionian Sea'.[39] After Agrippa's death, Tiberius had followed suit in 6 BCE, despatched by his stepfather to keep in check an increasingly restless Armenia. However, Tiberius never reached his intended goal – midway through the journey he renounced his powers and went into self-imposed exile on the island of Rhodes, to live as a private citizen, though he did eventually return to Rome in 4 CE.[40]

The closest precedent to Germanicus' mission, both in terms of time and accomplishments, however, is the one undertaken by Gaius Caesar between 2 BCE and 4 CE. Gaius was Agrippa and Julia the Elder's eldest son and, together with his younger brother Lucius, had been adopted by his grandfather Augustus, thus arriving precipitately on the political scene as the emperor's prospective heir.[41] Gaius journeyed to a wide range of destinations, including Athens and Troy. In Syria, he was elected consul and was visited by the then Armenian king.[42] He then held a meeting on an island in the middle of the river Euphrates with the Parthian king Phraates IV to try to defuse the Armenian situation, thus preventing an actual war breaking out between Rome and Parthia.[43] The compromise saw Gaius establishing Ariobarzanes, a vassal of the Parthian ruler, as the new Armenian king; on the other hand, Armenia would have remained under Rome's sphere of influence.[44] However good the treaty may have been, an anti-Roman war broke out in Armenia soon afterwards anyway and, although the Romans succeeded in restoring order, Gaius himself was badly wounded and died on his way back to Rome.[45]

Put in this perspective, Germanicus' journey shows much more continuity with his predecessors' rather than an oddity adduced to Tiberius' desire of disposing of him. Family links between the local dynasts and the Roman imperial house were common at this time and needed constant renewal, especially with the change of either the ruler or his intended heir.[46] There was an occurrence during the journey however, that according to the sources proved to be the final breakdown in the relationship between Germanicus and Tiberius. It happened on the final leg of the young prince's eastward tour, as he entered the land of the pharaohs.

Egypt – with just the mention of the name our emotions begin conjuring up a fascinating image of the arcane, the mysterious and the exotic. Two thousand years ago this land exerted the same attraction on other men: Alexander the Great, Julius Caesar, Mark Antony – all fell prey, one after the other, to the charms of the land of the pharaohs, each incapable of resisting the pull of its millenarian culture.

Germanicus himself was enraptured by his visit to Egypt. How could he not have been? He was a sensitive and educated man, attracted by the mysteries of the heavens and antiquity.[47] Some of his stops in the land of the Nile are recorded by Tacitus, whose source for these anecdotes had evidently wanted to establish another parallel between the young Roman and his illustrious predecessor, Alexander the Great.[48] Germanicus is said to have been particularly fascinated by the ruins of ancient Waset, which the Greco-Romans knew as Thebes (modern-day Luxor and Karnak); here he was captured by the *litterae Aegyptiae*, 'the hieroglyphical inscriptions which remained on the gigantic buildings, bearers of former opulence'.

Next, the young prince visited the Colossi of Memnon, statues then believed to represent the mythical Greek hero Memnon; the knowledge of whom these figures actually represented – the one who originally commissioned them, the great pharaoh Amenhotep III – having by that point been forgotten. The statues were quite mysterious as, 'when struck by sunrays [at dawn], they give back a vocal sound'. We know today that the trick was due to some displaced blocks in one of the figures which, due to an earthquake during the time of Augustus, had formed an inner cavity; when the rising sun hit the statue the humidity which had collected in the cavity during the night began to evaporate, generating a hissing sound which visitors in antiquity believed to be the Greek hero saluting his mother, Dawn.[49] Germanicus also visited the pyramids, 'proof of the rivalry and deeds of great kings' and the oasis of Fayum in Middle Egypt, and he travelled up to Elephantine (modern-day Aswan), the 'ultimate gate to the Roman empire'. Tacitus is clear that such 'wonders' captured the young man's soul.[50]

According to our sources, however, Germanicus' visit to Egypt represented a much more serious problem than a simple antiquarian tour: it constituted the final breakdown of trust between uncle and nephew. It seems that Tiberius 'harshly reprimanded Germanicus because he had entered Alexandria without the emperor's consent, against Augustus' dispositions.'[51] According to Suetonius, though, Germanicus seems to have gone to Egypt not to study antiquities, as Tacitus claims, but in response to 'a huge and sudden famine' there.[52] In order to better understand Tiberius' alleged anger, we need to analyse the special position that Egypt had among the provinces of the empire.

After Augustus' defeat of Mark Antony and Cleopatra in 30 BCE, following their suicide Egypt was annexed to the first emperor's private domains. This meant it was not to be treated like any other Roman province created before. The land of the pharaohs was to become a personal possession of the emperor and its administration was in the hands of the *praefectus Aegypti*, a member of the equestrian order directly subordinate to the *princeps*.[53] Egypt was also highly significant in that it represented 'Rome's granary': it was from here that the majority of the grain directed to the capital city came. Whoever controlled it had in his hands the power to soothe or to anger the people of Rome, who might rebel at any point if they were not fed on time. Such a delicate situation explains why Augustus had predisposed that no senator whatsoever should enter the province without explicit permission to do so from the first citizen himself. From our source's point of view Germanicus had violated this rule, incurring his uncle's wrath in consequence. However, we do need to take a step back before expressing any final judgement.

Before Germanicus' departure for the east, the Senate had bestowed upon the prince the *imperium maius*; a supreme power second only to the emperor's, which allowed the young prince to exert his authority over all those provinces 'which are divided by the sea'.[54] All the governors of such provinces were thus subjected to Germanicus' command.[55] Modern scholars, however, still debate on the opaque nature of these provinces 'divided by the sea'; which ones were they? And was Egypt to be considered as one of them?

Let us compare Germanicus' mission to the eastern tours of Agrippa and of Gaius Caesar discussed above. When describing Agrippa's travels, Josephus declares that all the provinces beyond the Ionian Sea were considered part of his *imperium*; he calls such provinces 'transmarine'.[56] When it comes to Gaius

Caesar, however, opinions diverge: some authors state that the young prince visited Egypt with Augustus' consent, whereas others argue that he went there without the emperor being aware of it. Whatever the case, Augustus did not reprimand his grandson and heir, in stark contrast with what happened years later between Tiberius and Germanicus. What to make of our prince, therefore? Did he consider Egypt to be part of the provinces under his jurisdiction or not?

Some elements seem to point towards an affirmative answer. We are fortunate enough to have a papyrus from the oasis of Fayum, in Middle Egypt, which contains the recorded text of a speech that Germanicus directed to the citizens of Alexandria, the province's main city.[57] In it, Germanicus refers to himself as Tiberius' envoy.[58] It is important to stress here the real motive for the young prince's visit to Egypt in the first place: even though Tacitus enjoys highlighting Germanicus' lust for antiquities, he also acknowledges (like Suetonius) that 'care for the province' because of an ongoing famine was the main reason for the prince's trip.[59] The famine may have been due to maladministration by the then prefect of Egypt, Lucius Seius Strabo, biological father of the future praetorian prefect Aelius Sejanus (see Chapter 4).[60] Perhaps Germanicus, being the *princeps'* stepson, thought that he did not need any formal authorization from Tiberius to enter the land of the Nile and could deal with matters in the east as he saw fit, by virtue of his *imperium maius* (but still, however, with respect to his uncle's authority). Or perhaps, due to the outbreak of famine, he reckoned that what mattered most was to act quickly, in order to prevent any uprising of the populace in Rome because of the lack of grain, which could also imperil Tiberius' position as first citizen. Sending a request to his uncle in Rome and waiting for an answer would indeed have cost him precious time during which the situation could have deteriorated rapidly.

Unfortunately, there is no absolute certainty over the real reason for which Germanicus journeyed to Egypt, seemingly unauthorized. However, there is one point worth stressing. In our literary sources, Tiberius complains about the fact that Germanicus entered Alexandria without his approval; the word Egypt is never mentioned. Why would the emperor have to be afraid of such a city? In the *Papyrus Oxyrhynchus XXV 2435*, while still addressing the inhabitants of Alexandria, Germanicus refused the divine honours the Alexandrians wanted to confer on him and his wife, claiming that if any such honour were due, it should be bestowed upon his uncle and the emperor's mother, the matriarch Livia.[61]

Perhaps for the first time here we can catch a glimpse of Germanicus' political vision: an idea of the principate akin to a Hellenistic kingdom, if he truly exhorted the inhabitants of Alexandria to acclaim Tiberius and Livia as living gods. This view would have been in contrast to the philo-senatorial politics of both Augustus and Tiberius, which rejected anything that could link the new political reality to a monarchy – something abhorrent in Rome, where kings had been exiled since the sixth century BCE. However, as we will see later, the fact that Germanicus made such a request of the Alexandrians may also be considered as part of his conciliatory politics towards local culture – a consistent trait of his way of working with non-Roman communities. Indeed, Egypt had long been used to a tradition where the ruler was considered a living god – a tradition which the Macedonian dynasty of the Ptolemies soon adopted after taking hold of the country in the wake of Alexander the Great's death. Tiberius himself, although rejecting divine worship, sometimes allowed cities in the eastern part of the empire to endow him with divine honours during his lifetime, especially if they were free cities.[62] This shows that the emperor was not averse to conciliating people by adopting local traditions, something that even Augustus had previously understood and done. Still this does not fully answer our question: why would Tiberius be worried about Germanicus visiting a city like Alexandria?

There is another possible reason the emperor may not have liked his heir's trip to the Egyptian capital – not because he was afraid of his nephew, but because he feared Germanicus' wife Agrippina and the influence she could exert upon her husband.[63] Agrippina would have been able to gather many supporters in the Hellenistic city and we will examine her role in more detail in the next section of this chapter.

In all this, there is an underlying point which cannot be questioned: if Germanicus had effectively entered Egypt 'illegally' – that is, against the emperor's expressed wish – such a serious act of insubordination would surely have provoked Tiberius' quick reaction and punishment. Interestingly, the historian Robin Seager has pointed out that in our extant sources there is no mention of any action taken by the prefect of Egypt against Germanicus. This fact plays a major role in supporting the thesis that everything took place within the bounds of legality and that perhaps Egypt was indeed part of those 'provinces across the seas' over which Germanicus had ultimate authority.[64] Historian Livia Capponi recently counter-argued that the reason why the then provincial prefect, Lucius Seius Strabo, is not mentioned by the sources is because he was not in Egypt at the time; in fact, he may have possibly died on the return journey from Rome to his province.[65] Although if this is correct it could weaken our hypothesis, we do not know of any formal letter that Tiberius sent to his nephew in which he might have rebuked him or, worse, recalled him to Rome. Instead, the emperor limited himself to complaining in the Senate that he had not been consulted by Germanicus prior to his trip.[66] If the prince had made such a false step, the emperor could at any time have taken from him the *imperium maius*; after all, had he not already done so when, at the end of the Rhine campaign of 15 CE, he had revoked Germanicus' *imperium proconsulare* and augurate?

In Suetonius' account, there is an interesting parallel with these events which may help to clarify the issue further.

Vespasian, declared emperor by his own troops in 69 CE, left his son Titus in charge of the war in Judea, which had proved to be a thorn in the side of the Romans since 66 CE. Whilst Vespasian was travelling to Rome to be formally installed as *princeps*, we read that the soldiers in Judea, 'in their congratulations, saluted Titus with the title of emperor'. The suspicion that Titus had ambitions to unseat his newly acclaimed father must have grown stronger when, 'after travelling to Alexandria [note the mention of this city again!], he wore a diadem at the consecration of the Apis bull at Memphis, in compliance with an ancient religious custom of the country.'[67] Despite this, Suetonius adds that 'there were some who misinterpreted the matter' – so if doubts existed about Titus' real intentions, why should the same not apply when it came to Germanicus? Suetonius' words indirectly reveal the existence of contrasting opinions circulating about the same event, opinions that differed according to the wider stance one wished to adopt. From such early views stemmed the first written records, which were reused by later authors who, in their turn, gave their own interpretation of the events. This is how facts can end up being distorted at times, especially when an author puts his own interests before accuracy; and that is probably how Germanicus' experience in Egypt should be understood.

Alongside the main reason of the prince's unauthorized entry into Egypt, Tacitus reports a second story of contention between the emperor and his nephew during the latter's time in the land of the pharaohs. According to this, the emperor 'had disapproved, with moderate words, of his [Germanicus'] behaviour and way of dressing himself' whilst abroad.[68] Yet Germanicus had actually shown similar behaviour on earlier occasions, whilst travelling around the region. For instance, when he had visited Athens, he had arranged to be preceded in the city by just one lictor, rather than the six prescribed for his consular rank.[69] When the king of the Nabateans (of the famed city of Petra) hosted a banquet in honour of the young prince and his wife, 'golden crowns of great weight [...] were offered to Germanicus and Agrippina.'[70] Should we believe that the young man, susceptible to the exotic, had suddenly forgotten the decorum required of every true Roman? It seems that there is more to that. Historian Bruno Gallotta argues that Germanicus 'adopted different kinds of behaviour in relation to the different localities he visited [...] in order to appease the locals by behaving in a way similar to their traditions and customs.'[71] To prove his point, Gallotta compares Germanicus' above-mentioned stay at Athens, where he was said to be 'sympathetic to the city', to the prince's visit to Troy, where he expressed 'Phrygian and anti-Hellenistic feelings'. It seems thus plausible that his request to the Alexandrians that they bestow divine honours upon Tiberius and Livia should be read in this way as well. Moreover, Germanicus' emollient behaviour had definitely not been exceptional; precedents were available. For instance, when Agrippa visited Herod the Great in Jerusalem in 15 BCE, he is reported to have offered a hecatomb – a typical sacrifice of 100 head of cattle – to Yahweh, thus fostering the goodwill of both the city's ruler and its inhabitants.[72]

If this was indeed the reason for which Germanicus behaved in such 'un-Roman' ways, it would constitute a powerful political weapon. And the results he achieved while in the east seem to point to its effectiveness too, proving once again that Tiberius had taken the right decision in entrusting his talented heir with such important matters. Germanicus brilliantly resolved the problem of Armenia which we mentioned at the beginning of this section – he crowned Zeno as king, heir to the king of Pontus, who since infancy 'had adopted Armenian manners and customs.' This made him popular with the local nobility (the troublesome Vonones was later quietly disposed of, as we shall explain in Chapter 3).[73] With this step, not only did Germanicus act 'according to the wishes of his father and the Senate'; he also gained the friendship of Artabanus, the king of Parthia, thus defusing the animosity which had previously simmered at the border between the two empires.[74] Next, Germanicus effectively reorganized the newly acquired territories of Cappadocia and Commagene, former client kingdoms which had passed into direct Roman rule on the death of their respective sovereigns. The prince also extended Rome's influence over the caravan city of Palmyra for the first time, where he erected statues of Tiberius, Drusus the Younger, and himself.[75]

If Germanicus had behaved with the same arrogance and disdain shown by Syria's governor of the time, Cnaeus Calpurnius Piso, it is unlikely he would have gained the favour of the native populations, who were used to a different style of government and power. Let us not forget that the Roman empire was a heterogeneous and multicultural polity, where the skill of adapting to each peculiar context was vital for the rule of any good governor, who could then promote integration with Rome. This did not mean giving up his own customs and traditional values but was, again, simply a very useful and effective political expedient. After all, Tiberius himself had had a similar attitude to that of Germanicus when he was in self-imposed exile on the island of Rhodes between 6 BCE and 4 CE. From Suetonius, we know that on Rhodes the future emperor, 'contenting himself with a small house, [...] led entirely a private life, sometime walking around the gymnasium with neither lictor nor herald, and returning the civilities of the Greeks as if they had all been on the same level. [...] He also gave up on the usual exercises, both equestrian and with weapons, and wore a cloak and sandals in the Greek fashion after taking off his native dress.'[76] It is true that in this case Tiberius had renounced any public position, living in a manner much different from Germanicus' position as effective representative of the emperor in the East. Nonetheless, this shows that Tiberius, if indeed he complained at all about Germanicus' conduct, may have disapproved of his nephew's behaviour because of the official position he held at the time, rather than because of the behaviour per se.

All the evidence thus seems to debunk the existence of any real, deep rift between Tiberius and Germanicus. There is no concrete proof of Tiberius' reaction against Germanicus' entry to Egypt beyond the words of our literary sources: Germanicus kept his *imperium maius* and the affinity he showed for local peoples proved politically useful. All these elements in turn should add up to a high improbability of Germanicus being murdered on his uncle's orders. Against this is the report that the emperor expressed concern about his nephew's visit to Alexandria. Why was he so anxious about it? As mentioned earlier it seems plausible that, if Tiberius was really afraid of anyone, it was not Germanicus but his own daughter-in-law, Agrippina. The love that this woman was said to have for her husband matched the resentment and scorn that she harboured for her father-in-law.

2.3 Agrippina: devoted wife, difficult daughter-in-law

We could rightly call Agrippina 'the last of the Julii' since she was the only direct descendant of Augustus still alive and free after the patriarch's death in 14 CE. Her brothers Gaius and Lucius Caesar had died while her grandfather was in power; her mother, Julia the Elder, and her younger brother, Agrippa Postumus, had died in exile in unclear circumstances, soon after Tiberius became the new *princeps*. Her elder sister, Julia the Younger, had been relegated to a barren island off the coast of Apulia in southern Italy, where she remained until her death in 28 CE. Too much pain to bear for a single heart it seems; a pain which gradually transformed itself into resentment towards the individuals Agrippina considered to be the real cause of her family's misfortune: her grandmother, Livia, and her uncle and father-in-law, Tiberius.

Tacitus mentions the existence of a deep resentment between the young woman and the matriarch Livia from the beginning of his *Annals*, though we should not forget that the Roman historian demonizes the figure of Livia constantly and enthusiastically.[77] However, Tacitus' claim may contain a kernel of truth. Agrippina's ill-feeling may be explained by Livia's show of contempt towards Augustus' only daughter and Agrippina's mother: Julia the Elder. To better understand the origins of Livia's bitterness and Agrippina's own political stance, we need first to analyse two ideological strains which, from the time of Julius Caesar until the end of the Julio-Claudian family in 68 CE, characterized the political existence of the dynasty, at times presenting scenes of hideous infighting among its members.

Julius Caesar had attempted to establish in Rome a monarchy in the style of those of the Hellenistic east and for this he was assassinated. His ideological inheritance was picked up by Mark Antony, along with his place in Cleopatra's bed. Beside Caesar, Antony's models were Alexander the Great and his Ptolemaic successors, the kings of Egypt and ancestors of Cleopatra. His ruling style was autocratic and underpinned by the support of the army and the people (in this case, to be understood as the inhabitants of the capital city). In order to achieve popularity, Antony modelled himself on Dionysus, the orgiastic and lustful god of wine and drunkenness. In foreign matters, he preferred aggression to diplomacy, especially towards the neighbouring Parthian empire. All these tenets – autocratic rule, support of the people and the soldiers, adoption of Dionysiac behaviour – were inherited by a faction which formed around Antony's son, Iullus Antony and Augustus' only daughter, Julia the Elder.[78]

To Caesar's and Antony's aspirations of divine kingship was opposed Augustus' 'compromise'. To appease the Roman aristocracy, Augustus devised a system which seamlessly maintained vestiges of the old Republican institutions even while power was actually taken away from them. By styling himself *princeps* rather than king, Augustus was able to achieve peace and put an end to the internecine conflicts which had hollowed out the Late Roman Republic. A similar policy of collaboration with the senators and appeasement was also adopted by Tiberius and, later on, by Claudius.[79]

Around 6 BCE, the clash between these two political ideologies was resurrected. Augustus decided to remove Iullus Antony and those close to him from positions of relevance in the administration, while advancing Tiberius.[80] Historian Mario Pani believes that the old emperor acted so because it was exactly around this time that a new circle was forming around Mark Antony's son and Augustus' daughter, who are said to have become lovers.[81] Thanks to Velleius Paterculus, we have the names of some of the members of this alleged circle: Quintius Crispinus; Appius Claudius; Sempronius Gracchus; one Scipio (probably a Cornelius).[82] Their family names – Appii, Sempronii, probably Cornelii – are very significant: individuals with such family names had already been ardent supporters of Mark Antony during his struggle against Augustus twenty years previously.[83] That some of their descendants and relatives were now supporting Antony's son shows that political (and ideological) loyalties tended to remain within a family. It was not the last time that this was to happen.

After the removal of Iullus Antony and his friends from the political scene, a rift emerged between Julia the Elder and Tiberius – her husband since Agrippa's death in 12 BCE. Around this time, Tiberius was given command of the eastern provinces of the empire but, as we have already mentioned, he ended up in self-imposed exile on the island of Rhodes. Julia the Elder remained behind. Also around this time Julia's two eldest sons, Gaius and Lucius Caesar, were hurled on to the political stage as Augustus' heirs. The boys, partly thanks to their mother's rank, enjoyed the support of the Roman plebs.

In 2 BCE a major scandal occurred. Iullus Antony was condemned to death and Julia the Elder was exiled by her own father, allegedly for indulging in multiple adulteries. It is now ascertained that there was more to this than a simple lesson in morality: scholars agree that a fully-fledged conspiracy had been organized by this 'Antonian/Julian faction' in order to unseat Augustus and, possibly, to advance Gaius Caesar to the throne.[84]

After the events of 2 BCE, the remnants of the Antonian/Julian faction then coalesced around Julia's eldest daughter, Julia the Younger, and her last remaining son, Agrippa Postumus. Though Augustus had initially advanced Agrippa Postumus as heir presumptive alongside Tiberius, in 6/7 CE the old patriarch exiled his grandson and relegated him to an island, in what are (and probably will remain) unclear circumstances. However, the way Agrippa Postumus is depicted in the sources – as an unstable, despicable and violent individual – is very typical of the manner in which political opponents were usually described by the winning faction (the emperors Caligula and Nero received similar treatment later on). We can infer the existence of something deeper than character as the cause of Agrippa Postumus' exile: perhaps the fact that he had become the new hope of the Antonian/Julian faction after Gaius Caesar's death in 4 CE.[85]

In 8 CE it was the turn of Julia the Younger to follow in her mother's footsteps. This may have been directly related to Agrippa Postumus' removal, although how is unclear. Augustus once again exiled a member of his family, and like her mother before her she was accused of adultery. Something, however, does not add up: among the condemned was Julia the Younger's husband, Aemilius Paullus. If this seems strange, given the nature of the charges, what follows may shed more light on the matter. Aemilius Paullus was related to the Scipio who had been part of Julia the Elder's circle; moreover, Paullus was also the nephew of Scribonia, Julia the Elder's mother (who, at this point, had followed her daughter into exile).[86] Further, one of Julia the Younger's alleged lovers, Junius Silanus, was related to another member of the Antonian/Julian faction, Appius Claudius – we know his mother was one Appia Claudia.[87] It should thus be clear how, once again, there was something more going on here than simple adultery. The faction was again quelled, but it did not take long for them to find a new leader and their aspiration for an oriental-style monarchy lived on.

Enter now Agrippina. After her older sister's exile in 8 CE, Agrippina became the new pole of attraction for all those surviving members of the old Antonian/Julian party (which, for ease of reading, will just be called Julian from now on). Being a woman, however, meant that Agrippina could not propose herself as a real alternative to Tiberius, who had by then succeeded her grandfather at the helm of the empire (although she certainly did not lack the courage and strength for that). The choice of a suitable replacement thus fell upon her husband, Germanicus. Thanks to his mother's blood, Germanicus was the perfect knot with which to bridge the old rivalry between the two families: his mother Antonia was daughter to both Octavia, Augustus' sister, and Mark Antony. Agrippina, however, forgot about something: on his father's side, Germanicus descended from the *gens Claudia*, Tiberius' own family. Moreover, the young prince had already been destined to succeed his uncle from the moment the old patriarch Augustus had decreed that Tiberius adopt him in 4 CE. As we have seen, Germanicus stayed loyal to his uncle and was probably clever enough to understand how the Julian party's autocratic view of the principate would have clashed with Tiberius' conservative, philo-senatorial politics.

Taking all this into account, it seems more plausible that those political ideas which the sources normally attribute to Germanicus may in effect have belonged to Agrippina and to the young couple's entourage; we should not forget that the latter was made up of people who had close family ties with some of the individuals once belonging to the intimate circles of the two Julias. For instance, among the couple's friends we find Aemilia Lepida and one Marcus Aemilius Lepidus, who had kinship ties with Aemilius Paullus, Julia the Younger's husband. Aemilia Lepida was also related to that Libo who was put on trial in 16 CE (of whom more later), while two of Aemilius Lepidus' children were married to offspring of Germanicus and Agrippina.[88] Another prominent member of this entourage was Publius Vitellius, the grandfather of the future emperor Vitellius. He belonged to one of a series of *familiae novae* (newly ennobled families, such as the Plautii, the Petronii and the Flavii) who were quite close to Germanicus and Agrippina and who, from the reign of Claudius onwards, played a larger and larger role on the political stage.[89] It was this 'circle of friends' who, after the prince's death, probably developed an image of Germanicus more in tune with their political ideology and further from the truth; we will see their reason for doing so in Chapter 4.

Let us focus for now on what Germanicus allegedly said to his wife moments before he died: 'He begged her to put aside her untamed courage [*ferocia*], to submit her spirit to fate's cruelty and, once back in Rome, not to irritate those stronger than herself with her ambition to climb even higher.'[90] Only close friends could have heard such words, if they had indeed ever been pronounced, and only they could have twisted what Germanicus said to his wife, if they had wanted to do so. However, this passage is very peculiar as it testifies to the existence of a rift within the imperial family; one which had Agrippina at its centre (rather than Germanicus) and which saw her opposed to the older members of the household, Livia and Tiberius. We shall see how such a rift could have developed by retracing some of the key events in Agrippina's life after Augustus' death in 14 CE.

At the time of the Rhine legions' rebellion, Agrippina was in Gaul beside her husband. We have already seen how Germanicus was treated by the mutineers at the camp; we cannot say that his wife was similarly treated. When the young prince decided to send Agrippina and their child Caligula away from the camp, to keep them safe, the same soldiers who had previously exhorted Germanicus to stab himself now begged Agrippina to stay: 'ashamed and overtaken by pity, they remembered her father, Agrippa, and her grandfather, Augustus; they thought about Drusus [the Elder], her father-in-law, and about her – [a woman]

famous for her fecundity and her illustrious virtue.'[91] According to Suetonius, it was also the sight of the little Caligula which appeased the soldiers.[92] What is interesting is that there is no mention of either Germanicus or Tiberius in these passages. That Julia the Elder's daughter may have exerted some kind of influence over the troops is shown by another of Tacitus' passages, in relation to the military campaign of 15 CE. We read that:

> if Agrippina had not prevented [the soldiers] from destroying the bridge over the Rhine river, there were those who would have dared to carry out such an infamous deed because of fear. But that woman, of such extraordinary character, assumed the duties of a general in those days; and she gave clothing and wound dressings to those soldiers who were in need of them. Pliny, author of a book about the Germanic wars, asserts that [Agrippina] stood at the edge of the bridge, offering her praises and her thanks to the returning legions. [...] By now Agrippina had far more influence on the army than any legate or general; a woman had suppressed the mutiny, which the name of the emperor himself had failed to suppress.[93]

How can we thus blame Tiberius for believing that 'hers could not be simple concerns, and that not only were the soldiers' spirits urged to go against external enemies'? Tiberius was right to be afraid of his daughter-in-law's strength and capabilities.[94]

In those same years (14–16 CE) two major, if somewhat hazy, events took place: the alleged conspiracy of Scribonius Libo, and the attempt to free Agrippa Postumus from his exile on the island of Pianosa, off the coast of Tuscany. The latter was linked to another troublesome incident: a revolt led by a slave named Clemens. All three events may be traced back to a so-called 'plan of Agrippina'.[95]

Libo was the nephew of Scribonia, second wife of Augustus, Julia the Elder's mother, and Agrippina's grandmother.[96]

Scribonia had accompanied Julia into exile after 2 BCE, but at the time of the events she was back in Rome, having survived her daughter. We know that Libo 'was charged with conspiring against the state'; he had allegedly been led to do so by the senator Firmius Cato, who had introduced him 'to the promises of the Chaldeans [priests from an area south of Babylon who were experts in dealing with the supernatural], to the rites of the magi and to the interpretation of dreams.'[97] These mystics had reminded Libo in ambiguous terms of the 'relevance of his kinship' and, according to Tacitus, had enticed him into conspiracy by encouraging him to think above his station. Might Agrippina have convinced her relative to avenge the wrongs done to his own aunt and cousin (that is, Agrippina's grandmother and mother respectively) by getting rid of Tiberius?

Libo is described as a 'thoughtless young man, of pleasant manners'; it is thus possible that he himself may not have harboured any ill intention against the emperor, let alone being the mastermind of a larger plan to dethrone him.[98] Still according to Tacitus, Tiberius could have put a stop to all this nonsense straight away, instead of which he promoted Libo to the praetorship, made his brother consul, and invited him to dinner. It was only when one Fulcinius Trio made the matter public that Tiberius was forced to give up what may have been a private enquiry into the matter and to adopt an impartial attitude.[99] The emperor remitted any decision to the Senate which, following the episode, decreed that 'all the astrologers and the magi be expelled from Italy.'[100] Such a decision demonstrates that the aldermen (and the emperor too, since such laws could not be passed without his – if only tacit – approval) were quite concerned about the destabilizing effect that prophecies and oracles could have on public order; but it may also hint at the existence of something more behind Libo's simple naivete. Let us not forget that the 'Julian party' based its whole political ideology on oriental ideas – ideas which were deeply embedded in the study of the stars. Moreover, since Germanicus had clearly refused at this point to take upon himself the mantle of main opponent to the Claudian branch of the family, the Julian party may have found in Libo his closest living substitute, Libo being nephew to Scribonia and cousin to Julia the Elder.[101] When read in this way, Libo's experience may simply be a repetition of what had happened to Agrippa Postumus. Eventually, Libo decided to commit suicide, but did so after consulting with his aunt Scribonia – another factor which hints to the existence of something more going on behind the façade of astrological omens.

While Libo was on trial in Rome, another calamity overshadowed Tiberius' early years as *princeps*. Soon after Augustus' death, we are informed that a plan was devised to take Agrippa Postumus away from his exile and send him 'to the armies in Germany'.[102] Clemens, the person in charge of the operation (and slave to Agrippa Postumus himself), was not able to achieve his goal in time, however. Tacitus does not hesitate to condemn Tiberius and Livia for the murder of Augustus' last living grandson.[103] Some scholars believe that it was Augustus himself who decreed Agrippa Postumus' death just before dying himself; this matter, however, is still much debated and a definitive answer will probably never be achieved.[104] What matters to us here is Tacitus' narrative intention. By inserting such a negative episode at the beginning of his account, the Roman historian intends to denigrate the figure of Tiberius from the very first pages, presenting him as a tyrant who inaugurated his rule by spilling innocent (and kin) blood. After Agrippa Postumus' death, his mother Julia the Elder apparently starved herself, 'devoid of any hope after the murder of her son'.[105] Very interestingly, some years before these events and while Augustus was still alive, two otherwise unknown individuals named Audasius and Epicadus had already tried to 'kidnap' both Julia the Elder and her son and to take them 'to the army'.[106] Unfortunately, we do not know anything more about this episode.

Let us now come back to the above-mentioned Clemens: after Agrippa Postumus' death, the young man 'hid away in some unknown place to grow his hair and beard; for in age and general appearance he was not unlike his master.'[107] Clemens then began to spread the rumour that Agrippa Postumus was still alive and, in so doing, he started gathering followers. Cassius Dio even reports that at some point Clemens 'marched on Rome in order to take back his grandfather's [that is, Agrippa Postumus' grandfather] domain.'[108] The outcome of the uprising was, nonetheless, null; Tiberius succeeded in capturing Clemens by deception and disposed of him in secret. With regard to our research, the sentence with which Tacitus concludes the narration of this short-lived revolt is very significant: 'and notwithstanding that many of the imperial household, as well as knights and senators, were said to have given him [Clemens/Agrippa Postumus] support with their wealth and advice, no investigation was made.'[109]

We need to reflect on that peculiar phrase that refers to 'many of the imperial household' (*multi e domo principis*), for it would have been very difficult for one single slave to have had the means to carry out such an operation and uprising. The same surely would apply to Audasius and Epicadus, who are said to have been men of low social standing. Everything points to the existence of a mastermind behind these events; someone who had the means and ability to organize them and to coordinate all the complexities (the attempts to free Julia the Elder and Agrippa Postumus were in fact carried out at the same time).[110] Moreover, the fact that Tiberius showed no desire to further investigate the affair could be indicative of the embarrassment that the emperor felt if he realized who was really behind the troubles – and his attitude towards Agrippina afterwards reveals who that mastermind may have been.

Mindful of these events, it is thus probable that, at the moment of sending Germanicus east, Tiberius and Livia may have decided it was necessary to have Agrippina supervised, so that she would be prevented from causing further trouble whilst away. Perhaps the so-called 'secret instructions' that Tiberius had allegedly given to Piso, along with the choice of the governor himself, may be understood in such a light. As we will see in the next chapter, Piso's conservatism overtly clashed with Agrippina and her party's 'orientalizing' idea of power. Moreover, Agrippina and her entourage would have found fertile ground in the east to achieve their political goals, since the countries they were about to visit were much more inclined to an autocratic and divine style of royal rule; the carefully balanced system devised by Augustus in Rome was alien to them. The east was the realm of kings and god-kings; that Agrippina had such an ideal of sovereignty is shown in a later passage of Tacitus, where she, by then widowed, reminds Tiberius that 'the spirit of the divine Augustus [at that time, a deified being] was not to be found in mute statues; she herself was the real image [of such divinity], the daughter of heavenly blood.'[111]

In this world of divine rulers, Germanicus could be compared to and associated with his grandfather Mark Antony or to the great Alexander, who had both travelled far and wide in those lands. Perhaps this was the real reason for Tiberius' complaint that Germanicus had entered Alexandria without notice; in this city, the embodiment of divine kingship par excellence, Agrippina would have been able to easily gather support and consent for her own political purposes, if only Germanicus had agreed to be her champion. Things did not go according to plan for Agrippina, however. Germanicus stayed loyal to his uncle until the very end, and the friction between the emperor and his heir was a posthumous creation which did not reflect their actual relationship. Nonetheless, Agrippina's ambition was not buried alongside her husband's ashes; once back in Rome, the young widow was ready to show her stepfather once again how strong Augustus' blood was.

Chapter 3

The Trial of the Century

'Some thought that Tiberius had given Piso secret instructions (*occulta mandata*)': Tacitus' passage has been a matter of speculation ever since it came out.[1] What kind of secret orders would Tiberius have given his governor, Piso? By artistically manipulating and arranging his materials, the masterful Roman historian implies that these instructions were somehow linked with the removal of Germanicus from the scene, although he is careful never to openly claim this. It is also true that Piso's 'unorthodox' behaviour towards Germanicus during his tour of the eastern empire, and shortly after the young prince's death, did nothing but convince others of the truth of such a claim.

The suggestion that Piso killed Germanicus does not necessarily mean that Tiberius ordered it, however. In fact, at one point Velleius Paterculus even asks himself what Tiberius could possibly have done to deserve Piso's hostility towards him.[2] The existence of such a statement written by someone who, for once, was contemporary to the events, clearly demonstrates that something does not add up. How could the giver of such secret instructions incur the animosity of his own helper? And why would Tiberius choose someone who clearly had something against him to 'assist' his young nephew in the east? Did Piso truly kill Germanicus? Or did someone else spray the poison?

3.1 One step back: why Piso?

We cannot answer all these questions without first introducing the man himself. Gaius Calpurnius Piso belonged to one of the oldest and noblest families of the old Republic, the *gens Calpurnia*. His grandfather had been a supporter of Catilina, whereas his father followed Brutus and Cassius after Julius Caesar's death, remaining politically aloof until Augustus offered him the consulate in 23 BCE.[3] Piso's grandfather, father and brother are all portrayed in the sources in a negative light, often accused of cruelty or savagery with terms such as *crudelitas* and *ferocia* (the same word which Tacitus used to describe Agrippina!).[4] They appear incapable of being generally ruled by others, and some examples will show how our Piso was no less so than his relatives.

Tacitus describes him as a man 'of violent nature and incapable of deference, of a pride inherited from his father.'[5] In fact, Piso was a man so proud of his noble origins that 'he could barely give precedence to Tiberius, whereas he looked down upon his [Tiberius'] children [i.e. Germanicus and Drusus the Younger] as far beneath him.' Moreover, it seems that Piso's pride was further fanned by 'the nobility and wealth of his wife, Plancina'.[6] Cassius Dio reports Piso's opposition to a motion against astrologers which had been introduced by Tiberius and his son Drusus the Younger.[7] In 15 CE, Piso allegedly embarrassed Tiberius in the Senate by stating that the emperor's presence there would cow the senators, not allowing them to vote freely (Tiberius was apparently 'shaken' by such an outspoken comment).[8] And even during his tenure as governor of Syria, we read that Piso 'made no secret of giving displeasure to either the father or the son.'[9]

In the light of such examples, a legitimate question arises: why did Tiberius choose as governor of Syria – one of the wealthiest provinces of the empire, home to four legions – someone who held him in such disregard? Why choose someone like this as *adiutor* (assistant) to Germanicus during his eastern tour?

To answer this question, we first need to start with the meaning of the word *adiutor* itself. Historian Frederick Drogula remarks that, 'in the late Republic, the term *adiutor* had conveyed the simple concept of "helper", and it eventually came to signify a range of lesser offices in Rome's bureaucracy, so the word does not in itself demonstrate that Piso was a trusted friend and agent of the emperor.'[10]

Second, we need to remind ourselves of the emperor's favourite political line: that vision of the principate as a political compromise with the aristocracy inherited by Augustus, but imbued with an even larger degree of deference and care towards the Senate and its decisional power. Let us also not forget that the shady institution established by Augustus was still in its infancy, and the *princeps*' power had not been entirely defined by that point. Historian Mario Pani notices that 'in the early principate, the hereditary strength of the aristocratic families allowed them to maintain their prestige and, thus, to keep relevant their role in the *princeps*' politics.'[11] Hence the device of a political line aiming to keep such potentially disruptive forces at bay by appeasing them and embedding them in the fabric of government.[12] Piso's contempt for the emperor, and for Germanicus during his stay in the eastern provinces, would have thus stemmed from his awareness of this pivotal point.

But let us come to the most pressing question: why would Tiberius put someone like Piso in charge of such a key province? First of all it is worth noticing that the emperor, on the eve of the trial against his governor, reminded the Senate, gathered in the portico of the temple of Apollo Palatine, that he 'had given Piso as collaborator (*adiutor*) to Germanicus upon the Senate's proposal.'[13] Even though Tiberius' opinion was surely considered before the final approval, it is worth taking this detail into account, as it is another proof of Tiberius' choice of ruling style – that is, governance beside the Roman elites rather than autocratic imposition.

Scholars are divided when it comes to deciding why Tiberius made Piso his final choice. The two main arguments, however, do not necessarily exclude each other; in fact, taken together, they can provide us with a better understanding of Tiberius' decision. According to some, the emperor's choice of the senator should be linked to his above-mentioned, philo-senatorial policy: here, a representative of the old Republican party would have been able to counterbalance the orientalizing disposition of Germanicus (or, rather, of Agrippina and their circle of friends).[14] The other argument has Tiberius appointing Piso as governor of Syria in order to gain the old senator's favour. We mentioned how Augustus had devised a policy of attracting antagonist senators over to his camp, bestowing favours on them in order to neutralize their political capital.[15] As in many other things, Tiberius just kept following his stepfather's policy; however, as Germanicus was loyal to his uncle, the young man would have been able to keep an eye on Piso too, just to make sure he would cause no trouble.[16] Germanicus was invested with the *imperium maius*; an authority which could overrule, if necessary, the power of a simple provincial governor.

That Piso's appointment was disjoined from Germanicus' investiture with the *imperium maius* in the east is further attested by a point of grammar. Fred Drogula noticed how Tacitus had used the pluperfect tense when describing Piso's succession to Creticus Silanus as governor of Syria; this change of grammatical tense implies that the substitution of governors had already happened *before* Germanicus' investiture with the *imperium maius*.[17] This is a key factor for our narrative, as it demolishes Tacitus' endeavour to link Tiberius' 'secret instructions' to Piso with Germanicus' death.

There is an additional element to the puzzle which should not be neglected: Tiberius' own *imperium*. The emperor's authority was acknowledged as being *maximum*, thus higher than Germanicus'. Tiberius may have simply wanted to have a representative next to his young nephew as a guarantor of the emperor's supreme authority.[18] And who better than Piso, who could in turn be monitored by Germanicus, in case the old nobleman decided to follow his family's tradition of going astray?

As we are unaware of a similar position being given to anyone else, the extent to which Piso interpreted his degree of autonomy is also a matter of argument. Where was the boundary, after all, in a political environment which was so fluid?

Beside Piso we find his wife Plancina, herself descended from a noble and wealthy family, and one of Livia's friends. We will examine this character more widely later on in the chapter, analysing what she might have done to please her illustrious friend. First, however, we are going to retrace Piso and Plancina's journey to the east beside Germanicus and Agrippina, shedding more light on a series of incidents which, if taken at face value, could indeed lead us to believe that it was they who eventually poisoned the young prince. But was this what truly happened?

3.2 The governor's 'precedents'

In Tacitus' narrative Piso's arrogance and swagger are constantly opposed to Germanicus' tolerance and patience. This characterization emerges quite early on during their journey eastwards. In Athens, Piso verbally attacked the fearful citizens with harsh words and covertly accused Germanicus for his 'orientalizing' attitude, such as the choice of walking around heralded by one lictor only. In contrast, the young prince, when Piso's ship was about to be wrecked in a storm near the island of Rhodes, sent triremes to rescue the governor. Yet even this act did not appease the old man; the day after, Piso left the island in a hurry, keen to take command of the Syrian legions to which he had been assigned. Nor could he have been said to be a model commander, either: once in control of the armies, he is reported to have relaxed discipline and to have encouraged 'idleness in the camps, licentiousness in the cities, and corruption'.[19] All this was promptly reported to Germanicus who, for the moment, let it pass. But matters were not to stay calm for long.

The first 'diplomatic incident' between the two characters happened when Germanicus ordered Piso to take part of his armies to Armenia, where the young prince himself was at the time; Piso ignored his superior's command. The two men then met at a place called Cyrrhus, where they held a brief talk, at the end of which they left in a state of 'overt hostility' towards each other. From that moment, Piso always appeared in a fierce, provocatory mood and in overt dissent with Germanicus. At the banquet organized by the Nabateans the old governor indignantly exclaimed that the feast was meant to be given 'to the son of a Roman prince, not for the son of the Parthian king.' He ranted about all the opulence and trappings characteristic of an oriental monarchy which the young prince was presented with. This too Germanicus endured in silence.[20]

We are thus witnessing a level of insolence on Piso's part which at times breached the threshold of insubordination. What could have allowed Piso to believe he could go unpunished with such an attitude? Perhaps the governor reckoned that he could rely on the support of a large sector of the Senate, rather than on Tiberius' favour.[21] At the same time, we must not forget that Germanicus' *imperium* had been conferred on him with the senators' approval.[22] Tacitus himself, however, gives an interesting clue: he states that it was Germanicus' friends (that same entourage that we met in the last chapter) who, 'aiming to foster resentment, twisted the truth by exaggerating falsehood.'[23] It is plausible that the extant literary works we read today used as their source that same twisted version of events that Tacitus refers to, which presents Piso in a completely negative light. What adds weight to such a hypothesis is the lack of any reference to the above-mentioned episodes in the case directed against Piso during his trial in 20 CE. Surely, if Piso had failed to send armies to Armenia at the direct order of Germanicus (who, let us stress again, held an *imperium* much higher than Piso's), the Senate would not have failed to register this among the main charges against the governor.

It is highly probable, however, that Piso's negative portrayal – exaggerated or not – is not the only supposed basis for his conflict with the young prince. According to the historian Felice Mercogliano, the juridical ambiguity of both Germanicus' and Piso's roles created constant confusion and misunderstandings between the two.[24] After all, no similar situation had arisen before. Mercogliano notes that, from the juridical statement preserved in the *senatus consultum de Cn. Pisone patre*, whereas Piso was said to be bound by Tiberius' *mandata* (orders), he was said to have received only *epistulae* (letters) from Germanicus. In other words, Piso would have felt he was subject to the emperor's will, but not to that of the young prince.[25]

At any rate, from low-level friction the relationship between prince and governor ended up becoming an outright political clash. The ultimate trigger was Germanicus' decision to send the former Armenian king, Vonones, away from Antioch. We have already mentioned this individual in the previous chapter, as being one of the main reasons that Germanicus had been sent eastwards by Tiberius – let us remind ourselves of who he was. Vonones was a Parthian prince who had been brought up in Rome. Some years before the events we are discussing, he had been made king of Parthia after his father's death and the civil war which followed that event. However, since his upbringing had made him practically alien to the traditions of his native country, the Parthian aristocracy chased him out of the kingdom, replacing him with his brother Artabanus. Vonones was welcomed in Armenia, where there was a power vacuum and the local notables made him king. After a short period, however, Vonones was called to Syria by the Roman governor Creticus Silanus, Piso's predecessor, who arrested him and kept him in custody. The governor acted in this manner to reassure Artabanus that Rome was not on his brother's side against him, thus hoping to defuse his threat to wage war on Rome.[26] When Piso replaced Silanus as governor of Syria, Vonones tried to gain his and his wife Plancina's favour 'with many services and gifts'. Aware of this, Germanicus relegated Vonones to the mountainous province of Cilicia in order to keep good relations with Artabanus. In fact, the Parthian king had asked the Roman prince that Vonones should not be allowed to remain in Syria 'so that he may not foster discord among the neighbouring peoples with his threats.'[27] Germanicus had been sent to the east to resolve matters, not to create new ones, so it is probable that Tiberius tacitly agreed with his nephew's decision to remove Vonones from Syria. After all, it was because of the authority conferred upon him by his uncle and the Senate that Germanicus had placed a new king upon the throne of Armenia in the first place.[28] In any case, there is no mention of any reproach from the emperor for Germanicus' decision. We can assume therefore, that the young prince did it not to spite Piso, as Tacitus would like us to believe, but in view of a bigger picture.

We can now examine what happened in the few months between Germanicus' return from Egypt and his death. Tacitus reports that as soon as he returned to Syria the young prince realized that 'the orders he had left for the [administration of] the legions and the cities had been either abolished or carried out contrary to his wishes.'[29] Piso had decided to leave Syria, but refrained when he heard the news of Germanicus' illness. Tacitus then records a series of events which, very probably, also belong to a historical tradition averse to Piso. According to him, the governor would have prevented the inhabitants of Antioch from celebrating the prince's recovery. When Germanicus fell ill again, 'Piso's envoys were accused of spying on the course of the [prince's] illness and his deterioration.'[30] Germanicus, convinced that he had been poisoned by the governor, sent Piso a letter with which 'he renounced his friendship; and many add that he ordered him to leave the province.' The aim behind the renunciation of friendship was to publicly state his displeasure.[31] Very interestingly, the *senatus consultum de Cn. Pisone patre* corroborates Tacitus' statement, adding that Germanicus believed the older governor to be the cause of his fatal condition.[32] Shortly afterwards Piso sailed away, 'moderating the navigation so that he could go back quickly to Syria once Germanicus' death had left the way free.'[33] When Germanicus finally did die, however, things began to unravel quickly.

3.3 Accusation, defence, verdict

The news of the young prince's death reached Piso and Plancina on the island of Cos, where they are said to have rejoiced at it. Piso's younger son Marcus immediately urged his father to go back to Rome and to submit to Tiberius' will. On the other hand, Piso's friend Domitius Celer advised him to go back to Syria and take back control of the legions there. After much pondering, the former governor opted for the latter's suggestion. In Syria, however, Piso's forces were quickly overcome by the new governor in charge, one Sentius; the only choice left for the proud statesman was to submit and return to Rome to await judgement.

* * *

At the fourth hour, the Tiber's banks were a kaleidoscope of massed crowds. The soothing and pungent smell of spices blended with the new perfumes just arrived from the East. The croaking shouts of the slave sellers mingled with the silk merchants' sweeter tones and the seamen's curses for those amphorae too heavy to unload. Among the river boats awaiting a free dock, a large bireme stood out proudly, like a peacock among a flock of hens. Its sails were flamboyantly coloured and loud laughter could be heard coming from the deck. The ship docked close by the Mausoleum of Augustus, of which the conical roof rose high above the wharf's storehouses. From the lowered gangway, Gnaeus Calpurnius Piso was beaming at a mob of his clients, who had gathered there to welcome him home with all the honours due to his rank. Just behind him, his wife Plancina stood, dispensing smiles to the crowd, wrapped in an apple-green tunic and with pearls shining in her fashionable hairdo. But the people closest to this radiant scene went suddenly quiet. Their eyes darted back and forth between the newly arrived grandees and the silent mass of the nearby Mausoleum, as they remembered the deeds of the young prince so recently laid to rest there. The two preening aristocrats, however, seemed to be oblivious. The jovial couple began to make their way to their accommodation, surrounded by their rowdy clients, without even deigning to glance at the tomb of their old rival. The initial surprise of those present quickly transformed itself into shouts of recrimination; the smiles and indifference would soon be wiped from the face of those scoundrels – so they promised themselves.

* * *

The day after his arrival in Rome, Piso was denounced to the consuls by an informer called Fulcinius Trio, who requested that the emperor should lead the upcoming trial. But Tiberius – who, according to Tacitus, was very well aware of the thorny nature of the issue – decided to leave the matter entirely in the Senate's hands.[34] The speech with which the *princeps* addressed the Senate on the eve of the trial sheds light upon traits of his character once again: Tiberius coolly reminded the assembled senators that he had agreed to send Piso to Syria as Germanicus' adjutant according to their own wish. The emperor recommended the aldermen to judge 'with a mind free from prejudice'; he exhorted the senators to move past the rivalry between the Pisonian faction and Germanicus' circle of friends and to strive for impartiality, to which he too committed himself.

After all, the emperor himself appears to have been sceptical of the whole affair, mentioning the possibility that some people were exaggerating certain facts and spreading lies.[35] Immediately after Germanicus' death the prince's friends had made sure that his body was exposed publicly, spreading the word that he had been poisoned. Moreover, they busied themselves in 'putting together the case for the prosecution as though the defendants were already committed for trial.'[36] In relation to this, Tacitus mentions for the first time one Martina, 'a notorious poisoner of that province and a favourite of Plancina'. We will examine this figure more closely in the next section; for now, we need to focus on why Tiberius is said to have been very annoyed by the spreading of such stories. Did he have something to hide? Perhaps Tiberius was afraid that the whole affair was yet another of the many attempts that the 'Julian party' had made to seize power. If Piso were found guilty of committing murder, having been ordered to do so by the *princeps* (let's not forget the *occulta mandata*, the 'secret instructions'), the armies and the people of Rome would have quickly risen against him for the love they had towards Germanicus, and Agrippina would have been able to see her dream come true.

Something unexpected now happened, however. 'It was related that Martina, the notorious poisoner who had been sent from Syria by the governor Sentius, had died suddenly at Brundisium and that poison had been discovered concealed in a knot of her hair, whereas her body showed no signs of suicide.'[37] How to explain this sudden death? Perhaps she really did kill herself or perhaps she was disposed of by someone close to Piso so that she could not reveal anything. But it might also be, since we have no factual evidence at all, that the same men who had asked for her to be sent to Rome – Publius Vitellius and one Veranius among others, who were also among Piso's accusers – were behind her murder, their aim being to make people believe that someone belonging to Piso's circle was behind it all. The latter option would have also constituted an additional, veiled attack on the emperor, given his alleged secret instructions to Piso.

Tiberius himself seems to have realized that something bigger was at stake: at the opening of the trial he urged the senators to pursue justice and not to mind 'Drusus' tears, or my sorrow, or the calumnies with which we may be assailed.'[38] That someone was trying to implicate him may be corroborated by the following passage too: 'a demand was made by the accusers for the production of certain alleged communications, but this was strenuously resisted by both Tiberius and Piso.'[39] Contrary to what his accusers intended (and to what Tacitus says), the senators seem to have been satisfied with the evidence provided by the emperor who, it is said, gave the Senate 'everything necessary for seeking out the truth'.[40]

Speculation aside, at the end of the trial the charge of murder was the only one to be dismissed, 'since not even the accusers could provide enough evidence for it.'[41] Furthermore the senators stated their scepticism, saying they believed that 'the remarkable restraint and forbearance of Germanicus Caesar were overborne by the savagery of the elder Piso's character and that, for this [reason], the dying Germanicus declared the elder Piso to be the cause of his death.'[42] The senators' decision should be proof enough that Piso was very probably not the one who poisoned Germanicus – and in consequence, Tiberius is freed from the accusation that he had been the mastermind behind such an evil plan.

Although Piso was cleared of the charge of murder he could certainly not rejoice, for there were even more serious charges which could not be disproved. The ex-governor was found guilty of stirring up both an Armenian and a Parthian war by his unwillingness to send Vonones away from Antioch.[43] He was accused of 'corrupting military discipline' among the Syrian legions by indulging soldiers and giving them donations 'in his own name from the funds of the *princeps*'.[44] And worst of all, Piso was found guilty of trying to foment civil war in Syria after Germanicus' death; the emperor himself had been 'inexorable' because of the infighting in the province.[45] But why had Piso decided on this course of action? What benefit could he possibly have gained from returning to Syria and retaking his seat as governor by force? It is worth going back to the moment Piso and Plancina received the news of Germanicus' death while they were on the island of Cos. Piso's friend Domitius Celer was said to have urged the ex-governor to return to the province thus: 'Are we [these are his words according to Tacitus' account] to make speed to land in Italy at the same hour as the remains of Germanicus, in order that the lamentations of Agrippina and the clamour of an ignorant mob may overwhelm you before you can even raise your voice in your own defence?'[46] But Piso's older son Marcus had urged his father to return to Rome as fast as he could – after all, 'up to the present no crime had been committed that was past forgiveness, and [he believed] his father had no cause to fear silly suspicions and baseless rumours; his quarrel with Germanicus had earned him hatred possibly, but not punishment.'[47]

These two passages indirectly testify to how quickly the charge of poisoning had spread after the death of the prince. The speed with which the news was disseminated; the lack of any concrete proof regarding the poisoning; the doubt assailing Piso and his entourage on what to do; these elements further substantiate the argument that Agrippina and her circle did exploit her husband's misfortune for their own purposes. Piso, however, had made a false step: the decision to go back to Syria instead of Rome (and the ensuing trouble he stirred up there) probably helped to consolidate belief in his guilt. While he was being besieged in a fortress by the troops of Sentius, the ex-governor declared that 'he, the representative of Caesar, was being excluded from the province which Caesar had given to him, not by the legions [...] but by Sentius, who was veiling his private hatred under false accusations.'[48] Perhaps events truly unfolded this way, the difference being that it was not only Sentius who privately hated Piso. However, the ex-governor's attempt to fight back only worsened his already precarious situation. His position should not surprise us; it perfectly tallies with his proverbial ill-temper and stubbornness, that typical family trait. If 'he could barely give precedence to Tiberius', how can we imagine that he would have given in to his opponents easily? But by such behaviour, Piso only ended up annoying Tiberius even more – so much so that he sent his son to Rome before the emperor in order to 'placate him'. This is further proof that the emperor and his governor had no secret agreement: if they had, surely Piso would not have needed to fear Tiberius' reaction.

Cleared on the count of murder, but charged with inciting sedition and military unrest, Piso went back to appeal to the assembled Senate one last time, urged on by his sons. There, he was met by the senators' renewed anger and accusations; though nothing seems to have terrified him more than the expressionless face of Tiberius.[49] It was the end: back home, after writing a letter to the *princeps* in which he declared his loyalty to him and asked him to clear his sons' name, Piso committed suicide; 'at dawn he was found with his throat cut, his sword lying on the floor.'[50] Some scholars argue that Piso did not kill himself, basing their theory on a passage of Tacitus: the historian claims that the ex-governor was killed by someone sent by the emperor after a letter had been disclosed to the Senate containing the famous 'secret instructions' that Tiberius had given Piso.[51] Even Tacitus, however, admits his doubts with regard to the veracity of this statement. Aside from all the evidence given above which debunks this theory, let us not forget that Piso belonged to a very conservative strain of the Roman aristocracy; for such proud people, suicide was definitely a much better end than suffering a death sentence.

In his letter to Tiberius, Piso begged the emperor to clear his sons' name. Tiberius agreed and Piso's elder son, Lucius, was allowed to retain his property provided that he changed his first name (it had been the same as his father's). Piso's possessions were equally distributed among his two sons; his statues and effigies were removed from public places and the household's women were forbidden to publicly mourn

ermanicus – Museo
cheologico della
aremma, Grosseto
uthor's own)

Tiberius – Musei Vaticani, Roma
(Author's own)

Livia Augusta – Ny Carlsberg Glyptotek
Copenhagen (Author's own)

ıtonia – Sackler
useum, Harvard
Vikimedia Commons/
blic domain)

ıreus of Caligula depicting his mother Agrippina on the obverse – RIC I Gaius 21
merican Numismatics Society)

Drusus the Younger – Museo Archeologico del
Maremma, Grosseto (Author's own)

Drusus Caesar, Germanicus' secon
son – Museo Archeologico della
Maremma, Grosseto (Author's ov

Nero Caesar, Germanicus' eldest son
National Archaeological Museum of
Tarragona (Wikimedia Commons/
public domain)

igula, Germanicus' third son – Ny
lsberg Glyptotek, Copenhagen
thor's own)

Claudius, Germanicus' brother – Musei
Vaticani, Roma (Author's own)

rippina the Younger, Germanicus' eldest
ghter – National Museum, Warsaw
rgererSF via Wikimedia
mmons/CC0 1.0 Universal)

Tabula Hebana – Museo Archeologico
della Maremma, Grosseto (Wikimedia
Commons/public domain)

Grand Camée de France – Bibliothèque Nationale de France, Paris (Wikimedia Commons/public domain)

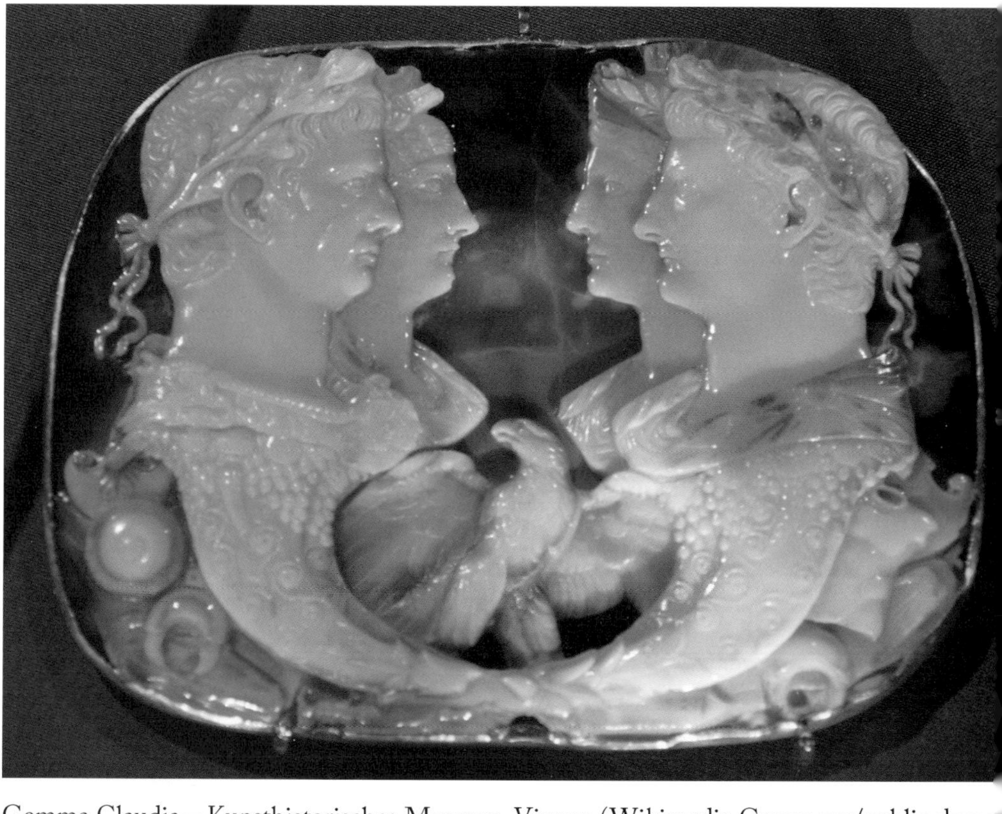

Gemma Claudia – Kunsthistorisches Museum, Vienna (Wikimedia Commons/public doma

I GAIUS 57 (American Numismatics Society)

I GAIUS
American
nismatics
ety)

I GAIUS
American
nismatics
ety)

Reverse of RIC I GAIUS 59 (American Numismatics Society)

Obverse of RIC I CLAUDIUS 103 (American Numismatics Society)

RIC I CLAUDIUS 105 (American Numismatics Society)

him.[52] Piso's house, however, was razed to the ground; by the end of the Republic such a punishment had come to be associated with charges of treason and of fomenting civil unrest.[53] According to historian Alison Cooley, Tiberius and the Senate took the opportunity to use Piso's example to teach a lesson to elites throughout the empire. By having the *senatus consultum* inscribed and displayed in every major city (the one we have is just one that survived), the emperor and the senators wanted to make clear what would happen to anyone (and, especially, any governor) who would threaten civil war against their authority.[54] By his actions, Piso had attacked not only Germanicus' life, but the *maiestas* of the *Domus Augusta* – the family who had by this time become the model of proper conduct for every worthy citizen.[55]

3.4 'Female treachery'?

It is now time to examine Piso's co-protagonist in this whole affair: his wife Plancina. I decided to separate their stories not only because at some point their destinies diverged, but also to better explore another hypothesis related to Germanicus' death. Admittedly, evidence for this theory is flimsy and scarce, but that does not mean it is worthless to investigate.

We need to return to the moment of Germanicus' departure for the east in 17 CE. Tacitus' narrative is very explicit: while Piso received 'secret instructions' from Tiberius, Livia 'induced Plancina to persecute Agrippina with feminine jealousy.'[56] Already in this passage we can see Tacitus' real intention: to suggest Plancina was merely a tool in Livia's hands, to be used against her granddaughter-in-law (we have already explored the grudge existing between the two women in the previous chapter). It must be stressed, however, that the first empress, as presented by Tacitus, is repeatedly denigrated. Livia is constantly (albeit often indirectly) depicted as the source of conspiracies and deception – a power-hungry woman who would stop at nothing to fulfil her ambitions. Although much of this negative portrayal has been convincingly disputed by multiple scholars, it has persisted.[57] That Tacitus' negative characterization of Livia may be just another of his literary expedients is also shown by his depiction of Agrippina. In total contrast to her grandmother, Agrippina, especially after her husband's death, is portrayed as martyr-like, a victim of Tiberius' and Livia's tyranny. It is very clear that Tacitus must have again used a source who was very hostile to the emperor and his mother – and who, in consequence, tended to enhance the qualities of all who opposed them. Whatever the truth, this ill-feeling between grandmother and granddaughter is the background against which all the events here described need to be considered.

Once in the east, Plancina seems to have executed Livia's alleged 'orders' to the letter. Not only did she start acting like Agrippina (with the legions, for instance, she attended cavalry exercises, something unusual for a woman); she also began to 'throw insults at Agrippina and Germanicus, without containing herself within the limits of female decorum.'[58] Such behaviour played a major role in making Germanicus believe that he was being murdered by the *adiutor* and his consort. Very interestingly, in that speech where the dying prince addressed his wife and circle of friends, he allegedly said the following: '[…] that I, the once happy survivor of so many wars, have now fallen by female treachery.' To whom was Germanicus referring here? To Plancina? Or his grandmother Livia?

We have already established the kind of strong bond which existed between Tiberius and his young heir; the relationship between grandmother and grandson must have not been very dissimilar. After all, Germanicus was the eldest son of that Drusus for whom Livia had once cried so much when she learned of his death.[59] We will probably never know for sure to whom Germanicus was referring when he spoke those words, if he really did say them. However, his friends busied themselves in spreading the rumour of his death by poison and sent to Rome the above-mentioned Martina, 'so dear to Plancina'. In the capital, meanwhile, it was already rumoured that 'all this situation was the effect of Augusta [i.e., Livia] and Plancina's secret conversations.'[60] To the negative presentation of the older matriarch was opposed that of Agrippina, 'a woman of princely lineage with her glorious marriage and used to being a subject of awe and gratification to the crowd'; she was the true model of feminine virtue, 'honour of the fatherland, only [living] descendant of Augustus, unique example of the old [virtue/customs].'[61] It is worth stressing again how these passages were probably manipulated with the intention, explicit or not, of denigrating the matriarch Livia.

Once in Rome, Plancina was put on trial together with her husband, but her story took a different course to her unfortunate consort's. Tacitus forewarns the reader that 'she was more highly favoured' than him; and then, 'once her pardon had been obtained through the secret intercession of Livia, she began to dissociate herself from her husband step by step and to treat her defence as a separate issue [from his].'[62] Even the *senatus consultum* confirms this astonishing detail for once: we read that Tiberius interceded for Plancina in front of the senators 'at his mother's request'.[63] When Piso understood how the tide of events was turning, he wrote to Tiberius and then committed suicide. In his letter to the emperor we are told that he 'added nothing about Plancina', while his own sons, when requested to appear before Tiberius to defend their mother, refused to do so.[64] What had Plancina done to deserve such treatment from her own family? Was it only her selfishness and instinct for self-preservation, or was there something more?

We talked about how the dying Germanicus believed that he had been murdered 'by female treachery'. Poison, a woman's weapon par excellence in antiquity, was considered the most deceitful tool to get rid of someone, since its effects could easily be mistaken for those of some illnesses: a work of 'treachery' indeed! Could this confirm that Plancina was the true mastermind behind Germanicus' death? She may have done so in order to spite her rival, making Agrippina suffer as profoundly as she loved her husband. Moreover, Germanicus' death meant the end of any dream of power that Agrippina may have had, since her means to achieve this had disappeared (although, as we shall see, Agrippina's ambition did not die along with her husband).[65]

If this is how events unfolded, it may have affected Livia's reputation – she who had tenaciously urged Tiberius to save her friend – and perhaps meant that the emperor felt deeply ashamed.[66] It was not the first time, however, that Livia had interfered with justice on behalf of a friend. In another example, her friend Urgulania was once summoned for trial by the senator Lucius Piso (unrelated to our Piso). Urgulania, however, did not obey but took refuge within the imperial house. Livia, complaining that Lucius Piso's act 'was an outrage and humiliation to herself', asked Tiberius to intercede on behalf of her friend to sort matters out.[67] That there are at least two recorded examples of similar behaviour by Livia is no coincidence. It goes back to the blurred boundaries that existed between public and private spheres in the early imperial period.[68] By the time Tacitus was writing, such boundaries had become well defined and it was very clear what an emperor could and could not do in the eyes of the public. But in the early years of the first century CE, the imperial family was just metamorphosing, from the most prominent of the aristocratic families in Rome into a ruling dynasty.

Historian Beth Severy explains this very well: 'In asking her son to protect her friend, Livia was operating within the family sphere; but because her son was the *princeps* and the imperial family a public institution, she was operating within the political sphere as well.'[69] The same can be said for Tiberius' intercession on behalf of his mother. Tiberius owed obedience to his mother's wishes as should any respectful son; at the same time, his position as the head of Roman society was very different to anyone else's. In other words, both the emperor and his mother were simply caught in a conflict of interests originating from the clash between the private nature of their household and the public institution that they represented.[70] To Tacitus this was simply anathema, such behaviours being filtered through the lens of his own time. From the early second century CE onwards it was highly inappropriate for an empress to interfere in public judicial proceedings, and the fact that Livia did so meant that somehow, in Tacitus' eyes, she had been up to no good and owed Plancina something. As far as we know, of course, Livia could have simply acted in good faith, believing that Plancina was guilty of nothing and thus employing all her influence to try to save her friend, as she had in the case of Urgulania.

After Tiberius interceded for her, even if reluctantly, 'all the honest people' began to fear that Plancina, as a free woman, would begin 'to turn those drugs and arts, now tested with such happy results, against Agrippina and her children, and so satiate this admirable grandmother and uncle with the blood of that whole unfortunate house.'[71] This passage too was probably sourced from the tradition hostile to Tiberius and Livia. Even if Plancina had truly murdered Germanicus, it is very difficult to believe that Livia would have ordered her to do so just to spite her granddaughter-in-law. After all, her affection for her beloved Drusus' son, Germanicus' steadfast loyalty to his uncle, and the young prince's importance in the state's apparatus must have counted well beyond any grudge that Livia, a true pragmatist and matriarch of the 'first' family, may have held against Agrippina.

So Plancina was given immunity after her trial – and Tiberius felt so ashamed (probably because it went beyond his absolute respect for custom) that he treated those accused along with her with exceptional leniency.[72] The 'honest' people's fears, even if true, never came to pass; after her acquittal our sources never mention Plancina again, except a brief note of her death in

Tacitus' *Annals*. In what is probably another literary masterstroke (or perhaps a true coincidence), Tacitus records that Plancina committed suicide in the same year in which her great rival Agrippina died (33 CE). Cassius Dio adds that Tiberius had let her live so that Agrippina might not rejoice at her death; probably another passage to add to the many belonging to the hostile tradition towards the emperor.[73] Tacitus provides us with a final epitaph on this colourful, if shady, individual's life: 'When both hatred and favour ceased, justice prevailed: accused of very well-known crimes, she paid by her own hand a penalty more overdue than undeserved.'[74]

* * *

What did the trial of the century prove in the end? It surely proved that Piso paid the price for abusing his position of governor and for stirring up trouble in his province. But it also showed that his was not the hand behind Germanicus' death. In consequence, any accusation aimed at Tiberius, implicit or not, as being the real killer of his nephew simply does not hold up. Plancina might have killed the young prince, but the evidence we have is flimsy and inconclusive – what we can be quite sure of is that Livia did not order her to do so. All these events seem to have been carefully arranged and retold in order to throw a negative light on the imperial couple. 'Instrumentalizing' events and shaping other people's memory is nothing new, nor is it unusual; such manipulation of the facts is exactly what happened to Germanicus while he lived and even more so after his death, as we shall now see.

Chapter 4

The Weight of Memory

Our own understanding of Germanicus' character and life largely derives from the ways in which his memory was shaped after the prince's death; our knowledge of who Germanicus was is partially filtered through the views of others. Germanicus' image had already been exploited while he was still alive; this 'exploitation' of him by immediate family members only increased in the years after his death. The aims of these individuals differed but had something in common: to use Germanicus' memory and popularity to convey a specific political message to their audiences. In so doing, at times they offered a view on the now-departed prince which probably had nothing to do with the 'real' Germanicus himself.

In this chapter we will see how the young prince's image was shaped – alongside his brother Drusus the Younger's – first by his uncle Tiberius, in order to make a clear political and dynastic statement. We will then see how Agrippina clung to her husband's memory to persevere in her political schemes one last time. We will analyse the ways in which Caligula commemorated his father to appeal to the masses, and how Claudius remembered his brother in order to boost his precarious legitimacy – an element due to his unusual accession to power. Finally, we will have a glimpse of the stress that Agrippina the Younger, worthy daughter of her namesake mother, put on her ancestry to forward her and her son's political position so as to finally achieve the imperial throne.

4.1 Two loyal brothers

Drusus could not believe the messenger. He stared at a sparrow which was lazily picking at the grass, sure of finding insects by the newly planted bushes. 'Sir?', the messenger asked, confused. 'What shall I tell the emperor?'

What shall you tell the emperor, Drusus thought with sudden anger. What do you want to tell him? That I am alone now, that is what you can tell him. That my brother, my only brother, the man I trusted the most, the person who could best understand what it was like trying to live up to your ancestors' expectations... Drusus could not refrain from punching the column of the atrium just in front of him.

The messenger was caught offguard. 'Sir! Are you all right?!'

'No, I am not all right,' said Drusus, blood dripping down his knuckles. 'I shall never be all right again, do you understand?' The messenger looked almost in panic now, unsure of what to say. 'Tell my father I shall be with him soon. I just need to sort this out first,' he said, raising his right hand. 'Yessir,' the man replied, already half-turning towards the exit. Yes, go, it's best for you – you might have been next after this column, Drusus thought, sulkily. He was not ready to face his father, not yet. He was not ready to be told how even more important his life was right now. He could not bear the prospect, the idea that one day the empire would fall on his shoulders, without his brother's aid and guidance. He just could not think about it. The sparrow, seemingly satisfied, suddenly took a leap upwards and flew away from the opening in the atrium's roof. Two flaps of the wings and it was out of sight. 'How much I wish I could follow you,' Drusus sighed.

* * *

The literary sources revel in reminding us of how Tiberius allegedly tried at every turn to advance his biological son Drusus the Younger to the detriment of Germanicus. For instance, according to Tacitus, Tiberius recalled Germanicus from the Rhine so that he might leave some space for glory to his brother Drusus.[1] That the picture is hazy, however, is shown by a contradictory passage of Suetonius, in which the author states that Tiberius 'did not have any paternal care either for his biological son Drusus, or for his adoptive son Germanicus.'[2]

Luckily for us, by analysing other kinds of sources – inscriptions, coinage, archaeological materials – a very different picture of these familial relationships emerges. It becomes clear that Tiberius considered Germanicus and Drusus to be on an equal footing; the old emperor was preparing both to share the imperial burden, following an (unsuccessful) precedent first devised by Augustus.

Augustus had attempted to create a 'diarchy' (possibly based on the Republican sharing of power of the two consuls), when he realized that managing an empire was too large a task for a single pair of shoulders. Hence, his double adoption of Gaius and Lucius Caesar in 17 BCE; the two boys would have shared the rule of the empire as the next pair after the death of Augustus (the senior partner) and his collaborator Agrippa.[3] After the premature departure of his grandchildren, Augustus had created a new imperial 'doublet' with the adoption of Tiberius and Agrippa Postumus in 4 CE. That the old patriarch believed this system was what the empire required to function efficiently is shown by his order to Tiberius to adopt Germanicus in the same year; in this way Germanicus attained equal status to Tiberius' natural son, Drusus the Younger, forming the next imperial pair who would have succeeded Tiberius and Agrippa Postumus.[4] The removal of the latter in 6/7 CE created another imbalance, later amended by Tiberius becoming Augustus' junior partner; in consequence, his two young sons came to the forefront as the new potential heirs to the throne.

Already during the last decade of Augustus' reign, the two princes' careers shared remarkable similarities – proof of what

Augustus (and Tiberius, with him) had in store for them. Both Germanicus and Drusus were exempted from the praetorship and they were advanced for the consulship earlier than the usual required age of forty.[5] Later, after Augustus' death, Tiberius let five years pass between the two young men's respective first and second consulships. Moreover, the emperor assumed the consulship himself during each of his sons' second terms.[6] He became consul only three times during his 23-year reign and each time it was with a prospective heir: Germanicus in 18 CE, Drusus in 21 CE and Sejanus in 31 CE. This fact alone should be proof enough that partiality in political matters was far from Tiberius' mind. But to further corroborate the idea of 'dual inheritance' comes a passage of the *senatus consultum de Cn. Pisone patre*: here Tiberius is said to have grieved in a way which moved the senators very much, 'now that all his father's future hopes for guardianship of the state were now placed in one man only [i.e. Drusus the Younger].'[7]

The official stance of the imperial household in such matters is also reflected in Ovid's poems. In some verses written during his exile on the Black Sea, Ovid placed strong emphasis on the prospective dual rule of Germanicus and Drusus.[8] In another poem, the author confessed that, next to the statuettes of Tiberius and Livia on his altar, there was also one of Germanicus and one of Drusus.[9] As Ovid was trying to get his exile revoked, he would not have committed to writing anything that could have antagonized the emperor. Such lines would surely have annoyed Tiberius if he had truly wanted to advance his son Drusus at the expense of Germanicus.

Tiberius' impartiality and his political project find concrete testimony in the material remains of two identical arches placed at the entrances to the Suburra from the Forum of Augustus. A fragmentary inscription from Drusus' arch mentions his intervention in Illyria during the Pannonian revolt of 14 CE and commends both Germanicus' and Drusus' roles in bringing back peace to the empire. Based on this, we can safely assume that the arch of Germanicus – whose inscription has not been preserved – honoured the young prince's actions on the Rhine in 14 CE, mirroring those of his brother in the Balkans.[10]

Another testimony to the equal status of the brothers is shown by their association even in death. This was also reflected in Tiberius' behaviour; he did not stop attending to public business during Drusus' final illness and subsequent death (see Chapter 1). Identical honours to those of Germanicus were paid to Drusus in 23 CE, including a silver *imago clipeata* (portrait on a round shield) and a monumental arch.[11] Likewise, the thirty-fifth plebeian tribe of Rome dedicated two identical celebratory slabs – today recorded as *CIL VI 909* and *910* – to Germanicus and Drusus respectively, which are believed to have originally been placed on an arch situated between the Tiber and the Aventine.[12] But the most evocative proof of the brothers' equal status in their father's eyes is given by the so-called *Grand Camée de France* (see figure 13). This much discussed cameo piece showcases the imperial family during Tiberius' reign, at some point after Germanicus' death.[13] Given the high quality of the carving and materials used, the piece was definitely commissioned by someone belonging to the court environment – if not to the imperial household itself. The most common and accredited description gives Germanicus on the right and Drusus the Younger on the left, depicted in the upper register of the gem, flanking the Divus Augustus, semi-recumbent on Iulus/Ascanius, the progenitor of the *gens Iulia.*[14]

So far, we have analysed evidence from the 'centre' – monuments, honours and objects commissioned and/or produced in Rome by the elite. A great number of testimonials to the identical status of Germanicus and Drusus can also be gained from the provinces. Such testimonies are valuable as their commissioners, usually members of local aristocracies, would have not ordered anything which could have gone against the line held by the political centre in Rome – that is, the emperor and the Senate. On the contrary, since the usual reason for the commissioning of such monuments was to curry favour with Rome (an act referred to as *captatio benevolentiae*), these remains are invaluable proof of what the political centre upheld and deemed suitable.

From Rusellae, a romanized Etruscan town in today's southern Tuscany, comes the inscription of one Celer, a magistrate, dating from between 14 and 19 CE. He is referred to as 'prefect of Germanicus and Drusus Caesar'.[15] A monumental arch was dedicated to the brothers in another town, Spoletum, in modern-day Umbria,[16] while an inscription from another (now lost) monumental arch in Saintes, in the Aquitania region, refers to a statue of Tiberius erected there and flanked by statues of Germanicus and Drusus.[17] A similar setup existed in Palmyra, a caravan city in the Syrian desert which was brought within the Roman sphere of influence for the first time thanks to Germanicus. An inscription from a statuary group from the temple of Baal confirms the existence of another set of statues comprised of Tiberius, Germanicus and Drusus the Younger.[18] The same was done in Clazomene, a town on the Aegean Sea in western Turkey.[19] In Antioch of Pisidia, while Germanicus was still alive, statues of him and Drusus the Younger were placed on the flanks of the 'imperial triad' (Divus Augustus, Tiberius and Livia) along with depictions of the defunct Gaius and Lucius Caesar – a way to visually mark the link between the two imperial sets of heirs.[20] And in Olisipo, modern day Lisbon, an inscription confirms the existence of *flamines* (priests) dedicated to the joint cult of Germanicus and Drusus the Younger, at least for the provinces of Hispania and Gallia Narbonensis.[21] And not far away from Olisipo, on the bay of Gibraltar, the town of Carteia minted a series of *quadrantes* dated 18–19 CE in which Germanicus and Drusus the Younger once again appear together on the verso of the coins and are honoured by the town with the title of *quattuovir*.[22] Similarly, Colonia Romula minted a series, with Tiberius' head on the coin obverse and Germanicus and Drusus facing each other on the reverse.[23]

These various examples constitute just a tiny amount of what probably many other towns did to commemorate the two young princes, and whose memory is now lost to us. What matters, though, is that, from one end of the empire to the other, from Palmyra to Lisbon through Rome, Germanicus and Drusus the Younger stood as a pair between whom there was neither distinction nor favouritism – certainly not by the emperor, who projected an image of his two sons as equal future rulers of the empire.

But what about the relationship between the two brothers themselves? Were they jealous of each other – did each try to denigrate the other at the first opportunity? The literary sources are for once the first to suggest this was not the case. Tacitus unequivocally states that, among all the alleged infighting within the imperial household, 'the two brothers lived in exceptional harmony, unperturbed by the quarrels of their relatives.'[24] On his way east, Germanicus stopped over in Illyria to pay a visit to his brother rather than taking the more direct route from the port of Brundisium.[25] In his alleged dying speech, Germanicus urged his friends to tell both Tiberius and Drusus of his unfortunate end and, later, it was only Drusus – alongside Germanicus' biological brother Claudius – who went to meet Agrippina with the young prince's ashes on the way to Rome from Brundisium.[26] Drusus' pamphlet in honour of his dead brother was later carved into bronze along with Germanicus' posthumous honours.[27] That there was a natural bond between the two brothers is also testified by Drusus' behaviour towards Germanicus' offspring. Tiberius himself is said to have praised his biological son because of the 'paternal benevolence' he showed to his brother's children.[28]

Therefore, we can safely assume that the relationship between the two brothers was a healthy one. That Drusus may have truly cared for Germanicus' children may also be deduced from the fact that it was only after his own death in 23 CE that troubles for Germanicus' family began anew.

4.2 Agrippina vs Sejanus

After Germanicus' death, the young prince's memory was used by his widow and eldest sons as a banner to win over the people's love and to boost their political profile within the imperial household. However, the vicissitudes of Germanicus' family in the years 23–33 CE cannot be disentangled from the man who played a pivotal role in their misfortunes: Lucius Aelius Sejanus. An analysis of events thus first requires a brief overview of who Sejanus was and what brought him from a provincial backwater to become the closest voice in the Roman emperor's ear. His personality has been much maligned since his downfall, and it is very difficult to objectively reconstruct anything related to him. Bearing this in mind, some facts can nonetheless be carved out.

The first official mention we have of Sejanus is as adjutant of Gaius Caesar in the east, during his trip of 2 BCE–4 CE. However, we know that he was born in Volsinii, an ancient Etruscan town in modern-day northern Lazio, and that he came from an equestrian family. He was the son of Seius Strabo (see Chapter 2.2); later, he was adopted into the patrician *gens Aelia.*[29] It's in the east that Sejanus may have made his first acquaintance with Livilla, Germanicus' sister and wife of Gaius Caesar at that time – she later came to play a prominent role in the knight's life.[30] After the eastern trip, the next time Sejanus is mentioned in any official position is during the Pannonian revolt of 14 CE, when Tiberius despatched him alongside his son Drusus to quell the rioting in Illyria. By this date, Sejanus had already become praetorian prefect alongside his father, while his maternal uncle, Junius Blaesus, was in charge of the three Pannonian legions.[31] Given the importance of such positions, it is clear that Sejanus and his family had somehow gained the emperor's trust by this point.

The first change in the imperial household after Germanicus' death happened in 23 CE, when Drusus the Younger himself died. Drusus had become Tiberius' main heir and designated successor, especially after attaining the *tribunicia potestas* in 22 CE.[32] According to Tacitus, the people of Rome were worried about this, as it would have meant that Germanicus' family would be relegated to the (political) background – and the effect was reinforced when Drusus and Livilla, who had married after Gaius Caesar's death, had male twins.[33] We have already discussed how Tacitus' original source was probably biased towards Germanicus' family; but what demonstrates that this was an unsubstantiated fear (if, indeed, it existed) is Tiberius' own treatment of his nephew's offspring. Nero and Drusus Caesar, Germanicus' two eldest sons, received identical honours to those that the late Augustus had given to his own prospective heirs, Gaius and Lucius Caesar – and also identical to what Tiberius had done for his two sons. The privileges included exemption from the *vigintiviratus* (commission of 20 municipal administrators) and the assumption of the quaestorship five years earlier than the age established by law. Conferring such advantages confirms the emperor's intention to present his two eldest grandsons as his future heirs; this new imperial pair would take the helm of the empire after the passing of Tiberius and Drusus the Younger – who, after the loss of his brother, had effectively become his father's junior partner.[34]

After Drusus' death, the 'dual' system of power was once again thrown into question. This is when Sejanus reappears. We know that his daughter was promised in marriage to Claudius' son and that Tiberius made him praetor and 'advisor and minister in all matters of government'.[35] In this context, Sejanus may be seen as a sort of 'colleague' to Tiberius in government, one who could have acted as tutor to the emperor's young and inexperienced successors had the *princeps* suddenly died (let us not forget that the 'old' emperor was by then over sixty, a venerable age for the time). Velleius Paterculus himself calls Sejanus *adiutor* to Tiberius.[36] But why would the aristocratic emperor have allowed such a low-ranked individual to rise so high? Was there no one better qualified than Sejanus to act as possible tutor to the young princes? Some historians believe that because Sejanus was an equestrian the succession of the Julio-Claudian family was actually safer, since the praetorian prefect could not have made a claim to power based on his rank, nobility or family connections.[37] Sejanus would have thus been a competent, experienced and safe pair of hands to look after the stewardship of the empire in case of the emperor's sudden death. However, Tiberius did not die, and events took a different course to those he expected.

The first issue arose with the death of Drusus the Younger. The ancient sources claim that the prince was poisoned by his wife Livilla with Sejanus' connivance, as the two were allegedly lovers.[38] The sources also impute this to Sejanus' hunger for power and see it as the first step of his plan to eventually replace Tiberius. However, of this alleged poisoning there is no concrete evidence and, very similar to what happened after Germanicus' death, it seems to have been a construction *a posteriori*.[39] It is credible, nonetheless, that Sejanus may have strived to become a sort of 'protector of the realm' rather than actual emperor; his low birth and the alleged aversion that the plebs had for him would have prevented him keeping power for long, even in the unlikely event he had obtained it.[40]

There is, however, an incoherence: the sources tell us that instead of trying to become the tutor of Germanicus' sons – the current prospective heirs – Sejanus set his sights on the infant twins of the deceased Drusus. In order to achieve his goal, Sejanus asked Tiberius if he could marry Livilla, who may have agreed with this plan of the praetorian prefect as it would improve the chances of succession for her own infants over Agrippina's.[41] Tiberius allegedly replied that it was up to

Livilla herself to decide whether to marry him.[42] The fact that she did not do so, especially given her alleged keenness, raises some questions. It may be that Tiberius maintained the same attitude towards Livilla as he did towards Agrippina, whose dreams, now that Drusus the Younger had exited the stage, finally stood a chance of coming true.

According to Tacitus, following Germanicus' death Agrippina began to be *dominandi avida* – that is, 'greedy to rule/dominate'. Historian Francesca Cenerini has noted that such an attitude went against the male parameters of correct female behaviour that every respectable Roman woman should uphold.[43] In his alleged answer to Sejanus regarding marriage to Livilla, Tiberius is said to have had an additional ulterior motive for the refusal: Sejanus and Livilla's wedding would have exacerbated 'Agrippina's resentment, which would have increased even more as Livilla's wedding would have torn the imperial household into two opposing factions. Such was the rivalry between the two women that even his [Tiberius'] grandsons were affected by it.'[44] Anything that would imperil political stability was anathema to Tiberius and the birth of an additional potential heir to the throne from a re-marriage of Livilla (or Agrippina, as we shall see) could have jeopardized the already fragile succession that the emperor had striven to uphold.[45]

There is enough evidence to believe that Nero and Drusus Caesar were initially considered by Tiberius as his true prospective heirs, especially after Drusus the Younger's death. In the Senate, Tiberius introduced the two young princes as the 'only relief to our current misfortunes' and appealed to the senators to take care of the two boys.[46] On the already mentioned *Grand Camée de France*, the two young princes figure prominently, though scholars disagree on which particular image represents which prince.[47] From Formiae, on the coast of modern-day Lazio, an inscription records the existence of a prefect of Nero and Drusus Caesar, in identical fashion to the inscription from Rusellae dedicated to Germanicus and Drusus the Younger discussed earlier.[48] Despite their position in the dynastic succession, however, Nero and Drusus Caesar were both out of the political scene (and out of life) in few years. What had brought Tiberius to change his plans and mind in such a short period of time? What had happened that could have justified risking the political stability he had always yearned for?

The years 23–31 saw the final downfall of Agrippina, of her two eldest sons and of some of her closest associates. Some scholars believe that Germanicus' widow was at the head of another 'pro-Julian' conspiracy aiming to replace Tiberius with Nero Caesar and that a series of trials against her collaborators which took place during these years were intended to thwart the peril.[49] Others argue that the trials were a preventative measure against possible conspiracy and that Sejanus acted as he did not out of power lust, but out of concern for the state and for the safeguarding of the emperor.[50] Yet a third faction believes that Sejanus simply wanted to exploit the fracture within the imperial family for his own political gains.[51] Whatever the reason, it is undeniable that there existed frictions between Tiberius (and Sejanus) on the one hand and Agrippina on the other, and that the attrition turned into an open conflict which eventually put an end to Agrippina's possible aspirations once and for all.

The first to go was the *eques* Clutorius Priscus, even before Drusus the Younger's death. He had initially been rewarded by the emperor for composing a poem marking the passing of Germanicus.[52] However, he was later tried for *lesa maiestas* – an offence to the emperor's Roman sovereignty – following the accusation of a *delator*, an informer. Although Tiberius is often accused by the sources of relying on such *delatores*' spurious charges to get rid of his political opponents, nothing in Tacitus' narrative suggests that the emperor was guilty of injustice. Rather, it seems that it was the *delatores* who were exploiting pitfalls in the *lex maiestatis* to achieve their ends, and that Tiberius' only guilt lay in being blind to such tricks.[53]

In 24 CE it was the turn of Gaius Silius, 'for whom Germanicus' friendship was damaging', and his wife Sosia Galla, allegedly 'disliked by Tiberius because of Agrippina's affection for her'.[54] Interestingly, the friendship between Silius and Agrippina was not mentioned at all during Silius' trial; it seems plausible that the emperor's suspicions had been aroused by Sejanus' insistence on the potential danger that could come from Agrippina's party.[55]

In the same year Vibius Serenus, already in exile, was accused by his son of having sent people to stir up trouble in Gaul against the *princeps.*[56] Suillius, 'once quaestor to Germanicus', also went into exile and in 26 CE Claudia Pulcra, Agrippina's cousin, was sentenced to death for 'adultery and magical practices'.[57]

However, not every old friend of Germanicus and Agrippina followed the destiny of the widow's party. This shows that, if indeed there was a 'party' at any one time, allegiances could be fluid. The most visible case is the one of Publius Vitellius, who later became a loud supporter of Sejanus.[58] In 27–29 CE, another ex-associate, Vibius Marsus, was made proconsul of Africa – after having clearly distanced himself from Germanicus' widow.

In the same period, while its ranks were becoming thinner and thinner, Agrippina's party clung to the influence that Germanicus' popularity still had over the Roman mob. Moreover, they began to project the memory of the old Germanicus on to his firstborn son, Nero Caesar. This was so effective that when the senators once gathered to listen to the young man deliver a speech they were deeply moved, for 'the recent memory of the late Germanicus gave the impression of seeing him and hearing him in his young son.'[59] It seems that the greater the danger in which Nero found himself because of Sejanus' alleged hostility towards him, the greater the affection the people felt towards him.

In the meantime, a change had apparently come upon Agrippina too. Although she had not lost her old passion and arrogance, she was now referred to as an insecure and shaken individual, affected so much by the loss of her husband that historian Lorenzo Braccesi hypothesizes that she may have become clinically depressed.[60] Still, we need to remember how the literary sources – and, especially, Tacitus – do tend to depict Germanicus' family as victims of Tiberius' and Sejanus' tyranny, probably because of the pro-Germanicus source(s) that they had consulted (see above). It is nonetheless valuable to ponder on what Tacitus tells us about Agrippina at this time. In his words, 'after being affected by some illness [...] and after crying in silence for a long time, she began [to alternate] envy with prayers.'[61] This emotional instability, if real, may have been caused by the constant persecution of her friends and associates by Sejanus and his *delatores*. We have already discussed the dislike between Tiberius and his daughter-in-law, but it seems that the relationship soured even further as the 20s CE progressed. From a series of events recorded by Tacitus, it appears quite clear how the hostility between these two became more and more open and evident, till Sejanus decided to exploit it to achieve what may have been his ultimate goal all along. But was this final fracture due simply to Sejanus' interference or was Agrippina secretly planning something which justified the emperor's reaction?

In 24 CE, Tiberius became quite irate at the news that the city's pontiffs, 'in offering up their solemn prayers to the gods for the emperor's safety, commended Nero and Drusus Caesar too – an action prompted less by genuine affection towards the young princes and more by flattery.' In a speech to the senate, Tiberius 'warned that no one, in the future, should excite those impressionable young minds with excessive pride by loading them with premature honours.'[62] What was Tiberius worried about? Given Agrippina's past attitude towards her husband, perhaps the emperor was afraid that she might attempt to use her sons' position to achieve her political ambition in the same way she had tried to do with Germanicus. And would the two young boys stay loyal to the emperor as their father had done? Yet Tiberius' motive seems actually to have been more practical: he simply wanted to bring up his grandsons in his own footsteps, such a refusal of honours being typical of his philo-senatorial policy. The same sort of thing happened years later with Caligula, Agrippina's third son. Tiberius asked the Senate 'not to shower him [the young Caligula] with many an inopportune honour, so that he would not go astray in one way or another.'[63]

Some time later, in 26 CE, Agrippina, 'always irritable, and even more enraged by the danger in which that relative of hers [Claudia Pulcra] was', openly demanded that Tiberius stop persecuting the descendants of the divine Augustus. The emperor, with an 'unusual cry' (quite a striking phrase, given his proverbial calm and moderation!), rebuked her, saying that in truth she was offended not for that reason, but because she was not allowed to rule.'[64] And when Agrippina asked Tiberius, between tears and anger, to find her a new husband, the emperor 'left her with no answer, conscious of how important this matter was to the state.'[65] Although some scholars believe that Agrippina had begged for this in order to be freed from Sejanus' intention of marrying her, it is more plausible that the same reason for which Tiberius had not allowed Livilla to remarry applied to this case too – that is, to avoid the birth of any future heir of 'mixed' blood who might challenge the succession of the imperial household's heirs.[66]

Tension between the emperor and his daughter-in-law is said to have reached its climax during a banquet. Agrippina, 'despondent and imprudent', had apparently been informed by some of Sejanus' spies (pretending to be her friends) that

Tiberius was plotting to have her poisoned. During the banquet Agrippina did not touch any food and when the emperor offered her an apple – with no intention of poisoning her – she categorically refused to take it.[67]

Soon after this episode, Tiberius left Rome for the isle of Capri, off the coast of Naples in southern Italy, never to return to the capital. Although Tacitus states that the emperor's withdrawal to the tiny island was due to his desire to pursue his vices and cruelty with more secrecy, this does not entirely add up.[68] It seems more probable that Tiberius became tired of Rome and all its intrigues. The old *princeps* was already an introvert soul, used to looking for solitude and tranquillity as his previous self-imposed exile on Rhodes testifies.[69] The emperor had to continuously tolerate undue criticism from some senators and the servile attitude of others. He had to battle and deal with the infighting within his own household. His sons had died prematurely; his grandsons were too young and inexperienced to rule; and his daughters-in-law kept bickering, concerned only with their offspring's chances to rule rather than the future of the state. Agrippina kept challenging him, his mother Livia was quite overbearing and, in all this, Tiberius had an entire empire to govern. Who would not be tired? Getting away from Rome meant getting away from all the calumnies, the hostility and the hypocrisy. Whether rumours of what he was doing in Capri were true or not mattered little; people would have always found something to criticize or to gossip about, but now at least he could enjoy some peace in his old age.

Tiberius' departure, however, meant that Sejanus was left free to pursue his goals. If we follow the sources, this meant that he was able to effect the downfall of Germanicus' family. Scholars have debated on the extent to which Tiberius knew of and consented to his praetorian prefect's plans; the only thing that can be ascertained is that Sejanus represented Tiberius' main communication channel with Rome after the emperor's departure for Capri.

With Tiberius gone, the sources tell us that Sejanus quickly moved to attack Nero Caesar, Germanicus' eldest son. Before analysing events in more detail, however, it is worth noting that Sejanus did not carry out his final plan until Livia was dead. As the family matriarch, Augustus' widow would have not allowed anything to happen to her late husband's descendants, even Agrippina. The stability of the state which Augustus had spent decades to achieve could not be compromised. Before 29 CE, therefore, Sejanus limited himself to having a network of spies to spread rumours in preparation for a proper attack.

Historian Tracy Deline has proved that the chronology of the two main accusations against Nero Caesar and his mother Agrippina as featured in Tacitus' narrative should be reversed.[70] In 27 CE, in a letter to the Senate, Tiberius himself appears to have accused his grandson of 'unchastity and of loving young boys' and his daughter-in-law of 'talking arrogantly and refusing to obey'. It seems that the emperor used 'ambiguous language', as usual.[71] As consequence of this, Agrippina and Nero Caesar were placed under house arrest, probably in Herculaneum.

* * *

'Is everything all right, domina?' Claudia's voice reached Agrippina's ears as if from a distant land. She was too enraptured by the different hues that the setting sun was giving to the calm sea. An explosion of colours, which reminded the widow of the Nabatean dresses she had been given as a gift an eternity ago, when her husband was still alive. 'Germanicus…how different would life be if you were still here?' The emptiness in her heart had never left Agrippina since the day her beloved soulmate had left her side. Nothing had been able to repair it, nothing. Only anger was left now. And vengeance.

'The time is ripe, Claudia. Prepare yourself.' Her servant stared at her, confused. How could she understand, after all? Everything Agrippina had done, she had done under cover. No one who was not absolutely essential to carry out the plan was to know. The risk was too high.

'It is time to change my dress, don't you think? I fancy something colourful for once, as a change.' Claudia's eyes cleared. Confident now that she understood, she left the room with a smile on her lips, happy that her mistress could see the value of life for once. Agrippina turned towards the sunset again. Purple was king of the sky now, 'and purple I shall have,' she murmured.

* * *

In 29 CE, after Livia's death, grave accusations were made once more against Agrippina and her eldest son. Velleius states that 'the grief, the indignation and shame he [Tiberius] was forced to suffer through his daughter-in-law and his grandson […] were crowned by the loss of his mother', showing once again Livia's pivotal role in protecting the whole family.[72] Tacitus reports that Nero Caesar's guilt lay in 'proud and incautious words' which spies around him – allegedly including his wife Julia, daughter of Drusus the Younger and Livilla – had reported back to Sejanus.[73] The praetorian prefect is also said to have set Drusus Caesar, Germanicus' second son, against his older brother, 'with the hope of empire […] and because his mother Agrippina favoured his brother Nero Caesar.'[74] We can only hypothesize about the veracity of such an accusation. It seems plausible that Agrippina preferred Nero Caesar to Drusus as the elder son seems to have been more malleable, more similar to his father. Drusus Caesar, on the other hand, comes across as an ambitious and arrogant young man, much more like his mother and, because of this, probably more difficult for her to control.

In those frantic days, Tacitus describes how an air of revolt took over Rome:

> the people, carrying Agrippina's and Nero Caesar's statues, surrounded the Senate house and, cheering for Tiberius, shouted that the letter was false and that it was contrary to the emperor's wish that destruction was plotted against his house. [...] What remained but to take up arms and, in the persons whose effigies they had followed as their ensigns, to choose their generals and their princes?

At this point, Tacitus' narration sadly breaks off. However, something reported by Suetonius may help to clarify the situation. The author says that Tiberius accused Agrippina 'of wanting to take refuge by the statue of Augustus or by the legions.'[75] It would not have been the first time that Agrippina sought to use her antecedents and her popularity with the armies and the people to achieve her goals (see Chapter 2). After all, the 'Julian' faction's power base were the soldiers and the Roman mob. It is highly probable that the legions mentioned by Suetonius were those armies on the Rhine, where memories of Germanicus and Agrippina were still very much alive. Agrippina could thus have planned to overthrow the emperor and replace him with her elder son. It may also explain why Tiberius, long after Sejanus' fall in 31 CE, left her in exile on Pandataria, the same island where her mother Julia the Elder had been sent thirty years before – only by being sent far away would Agrippina have finally ceased to be a threat to the stability of the state.

After these somewhat hazy events, Sejanus' power reached its apex: he moved against his previous ally, Drusus Caesar, allegedly with the help of the young boy's wife (again).[76] Nero and Drusus Caesar were declared 'enemies of the state'; the first was sent into exile, while the second was imprisoned under the Palatine palace.[77] That events happened as they did was thus obviously not because of Tiberius' cruel treatment of Germanicus' house. This view is supported by the favour that the old emperor felt for Agrippina's third son, Gaius Caesar

(Caligula), who ended up inheriting the throne after his grandfather's death – notwithstanding the fact that, by that point, Tiberius also had a grandson from his son Drusus (one of the twins previously mentioned). According to Cassius Dio, Tiberius favoured the youngster to counterbalance Sejanus' uncontrolled power – by this stage the relationship between the emperor and his *adiutor* had broken up. Caligula was the perfect candidate, not only because he was the most suitable choice in terms of seniority, but also because he was adored by the people 'thanks to the memory of his father Germanicus'.[78] At least this time Germanicus' name was some help to one of his sons!

This is not the right place to examine in depth what could have led Tiberius to remove his praetorian prefect from power in 31 CE. Apparently the emperor, in his own (now lost) autobiography, is reported to have moved against Sejanus after realizing the existence of the prefect's plot against the sons of Germanicus.[79] This may simply reflect the 'official' version of events that the government wanted to convey. As we mentioned earlier (see Chapter 1), it was Antonia, Germanicus' mother, who revealed to Tiberius the scale of Sejanus' plans. Not every scholar agrees with this account – some see Antonia's intervention as fictional.[80] The majority do seem to agree, though, that Sejanus' fall was ultimately due to the opposition of a powerful group of aristocrats who could not tolerate that a simple knight had achieved such eminence.[81]

What interests us here, however, is the fate of Germanicus' widow and older sons. Soon after being sent into exile, Nero Caesar died, allegedly having committed suicide.[82] Tacitus and Suetonius suggest that Agrippina too killed herself in 33 CE, soon after the death of her second son, Drusus Caesar (still imprisoned in the Palatine palace jail).[83] Agrippina's death is narrated in the same style as that of her mother, Julia the Elder, the latter having supposedly starved herself to death after hearing of the passing of her son, Agrippa Postumus. At one point, Tiberius seems to have contemplated freeing Drusus Caesar after Agrippina and Nero Caesar had been exiled. After all, being confined to the palace rather than sent into exile sounds more like a personal decision of the emperor's than a public sentence.[84] Still, Tiberius did not follow up his intention possibly because of the revelation of the prince's involvement with Sejanus after the prefect's downfall.[85]

In relation to Drusus Caesar, it is worth mentioning an episode which involved him indirectly. In 31 CE, when he had already been imprisoned, the provinces of Achaia and Asia were 'terrified' by a young man pretending to be Germanicus' second son – in a way reminiscent of what Clemens had done with Agrippa Postumus' memory in 16 CE (see Chapter 2).[86] From our sources we know that this 'false Drusus' was well received in the cities he visited and that his ultimate goal was to reach the 'paternal legions' in Syria, confident that Germanicus' still vivid memory and popularity in the region would have helped him to achieve his aims.

4.3 The later Julio-Claudians

At the death of Tiberius in 37 CE Caligula became the new emperor, as the eldest and most suitable Julian candidate alive. He initially adopted his cousin, Tiberius Gemellus, Tiberius' grandson by Drusus the Younger, as heir to the throne, but the boy died shortly afterwards in mysterious circumstances (sources naturally attribute the cause of his death to Caligula himself).[87] What is interesting, is that the idea of 'dual' accession to power was carried out in accordance with Tiberius' will: one last time the old emperor seems to have tried to bring about Augustus' ideal of power sharing between two *principes*.

After his mother's imprisonment in 27 CE Caligula had been raised by his great-grandmother Livia and then, following her death two years later, by his grandmother Antonia, Germanicus' mother. Caligula then spent some years with Tiberius in Capri and, when the old emperor passed away, it was he who delivered the funerary speech. From the very beginning of his principate, Caligula understood how powerful a tool the memory of his dead father could be: in the eulogy he delivered for Tiberius, he 'reminded the people of Augustus and Germanicus and entrusted himself to them.'[88] And he made sure to exploit it as much as he could. After all, out of six children, he had been the only one who could claim to have been present at both his father's main life events: the Rhine campaigns and the journey in the east.[89] Not only that, but even before the young boy began his rule, the inhabitants of Rome and the legions are said to have been thrilled by the prospect of his accession: 'for he had long been the object of expectation and desire for the greater part of the provincials and soldiers who had known him as a child, and for all the people of Rome, from their affection for the memory of Germanicus, his father, and compassion for a family that had been almost entirely destroyed.'[90]

Thus Caligula used his father's memory and popularity to gain favour with the plebs and with the army. After all, the whole ideology of the 'Julian faction' – which Caligula appropriated – was based on the approval of soldiers and citizens alike. Josephus reports that Caligula was said to be popular in Rome, especially with the soldiery, 'thanks to the admirable qualities of his father'.[91] Scholars, however, disagree on the source of Caligula's political ideology. Whom did he follow? Some argue that he derived the idea of an absolute monarchy from his mother, whereas others tend to see the phil-Hellenic house of his grandmother Antonia as its origin.[92] Caligula surely did not inherit this concept of power from his father – considering Germanicus' loyalty to Tiberius and his brother Drusus, it is highly likely that the dead prince had shared the old emperor's view of the principate rather than his wife's.

Germanicus' memory also helped the young *princeps* to secure approval beyond the borders of the empire. Artabanus, the Parthian king, 'who had always despised and hated Tiberius, asked Caligula for his friendship.'[93] The trump card of his father's name was even used by the young emperor to alter the calendar: September was changed to 'Germanicus', following an imperial tradition for which the old 'Quintilis' had been renamed July, after Julius Caesar, and 'Sextilis' had become August, after the late Augustus.[94] From this anecdote alone, we can see how conscious Caligula was of the magic that surrounded his father's name and how prompt he was to exploit it for his own political gains.

But Germanicus was not only a name to be waved like a banner by his son; he also remained a model to emulate. This is particularly evident in Caligula's decision to conduct a military expedition into German territory. There had been renewed (if minor) disturbance along the Rhine. Like his father twenty-five years earlier, in 39 CE Caligula took the unsettled legions beyond the great river and into German lands, to carry out a raid and raise the morale of his troops.[95] Unfortunately, the extant sources are too biased and fragmentary for us to understand this campaign any better.

Links between father and son were established in the arts too, with this same goal to remind viewers of Caligula's ancestry. Two posthumous portrait busts of Germanicus dating from his son's reign, one from Corinth, the other from modern-day Rostock, were made with this in mind. Associating father and son was so important for the commissioner of the statues that some of Germanicus' facial traits were even altered to better match those of his son.[96] But it is in Caligula's coinage that Germanicus' image takes centre stage. The most visually impactful series are the so-called *signis receptis* coins (figure 15).[97] The *dupondius* shows on the obverse Germanicus standing on a triumphal quadriga (chariot) with a winged victory depicted on it. On the reverse, the prince is shown fully armoured while saluting (implying there are troops assembled before him). Surrounding the figure we find the writing *signis recept(is) devictis Germ(anis)* – 'for the retrieval of the standards after defeating the Germans'. With the issue of this coinage Caligula's intent is quite obvious: to conjure up his father's retrieval of Varus' lost legionary eagles so that he himself would be associated with such glorious achievements (after all, Caligula had been with his parents in Germany at the time). Anyone looking at these coins would be reminded that military blood flowed in the young emperor's veins. The *princeps* made sure to stress the connection by also issuing a series of sesterces, where he is shown dressed and acting in the same way as his father on the dupondius.[98] Most interestingly, the latter is also one of two coin issues made by Caligula in which the image of the emperor is not shown at all.[99] The other is dedicated to the Divus Augustus. This fact should be enough evidence of the pivotal role that Germanicus' image and memory played in Caligula's political and artistic plans: after all, the young emperor's legitimate claim to the throne derived from his father, who had been Tiberius' heir.

The dynastic link is made explicit in a series of coins showing Germanicus' head on the obverse with the accompanying titulature *Ti(berii) August(i) f(ilius), divi Aug(usti) nepos* – 'son of Tiberius Augustus, grandson of the Divus Augustus' (figure 17). On the reverse, only Caligula's titles are present, but that is enough: by presenting Germanicus as his father and the heir to the two previous emperors, Caligula automatically focuses attention on himself and his newly acquired role.[100]

A variant of this series has Caligula's head on the obverse and Germanicus' on the reverse, accompanied by various titles (figure 16). These early coin issues parallel others showing other members of the imperial family on the reverse, such as Agrippina and the divine Augustus.[101] As these series date from quite early in Caligula's principate – they were mostly minted in the first year of his reign, 37–38 CE – the new emperor was again trying to prove his legitimacy to rule by stressing the bloodlinks with his forebears. This was particularly necessary as, in contrast to Tiberius at the time of Augustus' death, Germanicus' son was neither the old emperor's associate ruler nor his adopted heir: his subjects needed to be reminded why this young boy had the best claim to become the empire's new sovereign.

Despite initial popularity, heightened by the memories of Germanicus, Caligula was not able to retain power for long: after only four years of a reign made even more ambiguous by the scarcity of sources, the young emperor was assassinated in a military coup. What is clear, however, is that Caligula suffered the consequences of putting into practice his mother's – and the 'Julian' faction's – dream of a divine monarchy. Rome's nobility was not yet ready to abandon the successful 'Augustan compromise', so well maintained by Tiberius. And it was to a form of compromise that they returned.

Claudius, Germanicus' brother, was allegedly found hiding behind a curtain by some praetorians in the chaotic hours following Caligula's death. He was shuffled on to a litter, brought to the praetorian barracks at the edge of the city and, there, acclaimed emperor.[102] At least, this is what the extant sources want us to believe; modern studies have shown how Claudius' election was in truth the outcome of a shrewd plan between the man himself and the praetorians.[103] It may well be that, as Josephus states, the praetorians wanted to make Claudius emperor 'for the benevolence they held towards Germanicus, his brother'.[104] But it is clear that Claudius needed to try every means to affirm his legitimacy to rule.

In contrast with his two predecessors, Claudius had no direct relationship with the divine Augustus. Unlike Tiberius, he had never been formally adopted into the Julian family. True, his mother Antonia was the daughter of Octavia, Augustus' sister, but this could not compare to Caligula's direct blood link with the empire's founder. Moreover, Claudius had always been kept away from public office by his family, allegedly because of physical deformity and 'stupidity'.[105] However, as his literary achievements and his years of rule were to show, this man was anything but stupid.

Once elected *princeps*, Claudius had to prove that his newly acquired position was justified. To achieve this he exploited his family connections in a similar way to Caligula, at least initially. That Claudius needed such justification is exemplified by a passage of Tacitus, in relation to Piso's trial. At the end of the proceedings, the senator Valerius Messalinus asked that Tiberius, Livia, Antonia, Agrippina and Drusus the Younger be formally thanked for avenging Germanicus, without mentioning Claudius. Claudius' name was added only later, confirming how many had not even considered him to be in effect a member of the imperial household.[106] It was because of this that Claudius exploited the name of his brother, though in a less prominent way than Caligula had done. In fact, Claudius and Germanicus' own father, Drusus the Elder, is actually given a higher profile than Germanicus in Claudius' propagandist commissions.

Germanicus' name was added alongside those of other members of the family on an arch on the via Lata which celebrated Claudius' conquest of Britain.[107] And in an inscription found near Ponte Rotto, in central Rome, the new emperor and his brother are remembered together.[108] These are only two of the material testimonies of Claudius' use of his brother's memory to boost his status. The creation of such a visual link was extended to formal ceremonies. For instance, on his way to Britain in 43 CE, Claudius paid a visit to the monuments of remembrance dedicated to his father and brother on the Rhine. Here, on 10 October (the anniversary of Germanicus' death), in front of the troops, a commemorative ceremony was held; it is evident how the new emperor sought to draw a comparison between his sibling's military exploits and the one he himself was about to embark upon.[109] A similar tactic was adopted in the eastern part of the empire. In Syria, a region where Germanicus' memory was still strong, Claudius decided to found a new military colony named 'Germaniceia'.[110] Once again the new emperor made use of his brother's popularity to bolster the troops' loyalty towards himself. It is interesting that once his rulership had been consolidated, after the conquest of Britain in 43 CE, the emperor began to feel secure enough in his position as military commander and as a consequence of his new-found confidence depictions of Germanicus and Drusus the Elder were less in evidence.[111]

Germanicus does not appear as prominently on Claudius' coinage as on Caligula's. The only imperial series that we know of has Germanicus' head on the obverse of the coin, surrounded by his titles of Caesar, son of Tiberius and grandson of the Divus Augustus; on the reverse, Claudius' imperial titles appear, including the honorific title of 'Germanicus' (figure 20). From Cappadocia, however, comes an interesting series which presents Germanicus' memory in a local light. It is included in Caligula's coinage today, but there are grounds to believe it may have been minted early in Claudius' reign.[112] The reverse of this coin has two standing figures identified by the names of 'Artaxias' and 'Germanicus'. Germanicus is shown in the act of crowning Artaxias, who is none other than Zeno, the king of Armenia whom the young prince had crowned during his eastern tour of 18 CE (figure 18). It is clear how the region affirmed its loyalty to Rome by showcasing its most recent significant geopolitical act in the area. For these were indeed uncertain years, which could have resulted in major political changes. In 35 CE, at the end of Tiberius' reign, Zeno/Artaxias died; his exit from the scene created a power vacuum which the Parthians sought to exploit. His successor had been removed by Caligula, but Claudius decided to reinstate him, while also threatening war on Parthia.[113] The situation then settled down, with the emperor himself later exploiting the power vacuum created by the death of the Parthian king, but it is interesting that, at a time of doubt and uncertainty, Germanicus' figure was used by a local elite as a way to express their loyalty towards the imperial court in Rome.

Perhaps the greatest use Claudius made of his brother's memory (and legacy) was in taking the decision to marry Germanicus' last living daughter. In 48 CE Agrippina the Younger was indeed Germanicus' only living child – something she was herself acutely aware of, as we shall see later. In 48 CE Valeria Messalina, Claudius' third wife, died in ambiguous circumstances, allegedly while plotting to have her husband removed from the throne. In deciding on a new wife, Claudius was presented with a choice of candidates, amongst whom was his niece Agrippina the Younger, who also had the merit of 'bringing with her the grandson of Germanicus' – that is, the young Nero, son of her previous marriage to Lucius Domitius Aenobarbus.[114] That Germanicus' memory still played some part in swaying the emperor's decision at this point is shown by another comment of Tacitus about Nero, who is said to be favoured by the people 'for the memory of Germanicus, whose only male descendant he [Nero] was.'[115] In bringing Nero with her, Agrippina would have made sure that the 'Julian' and 'Claudian' branches of the family were finally amalgamated, by enabling Claudius to claim a direct link with the divine Augustus.

The most striking evidence of the legacy and legitimacy that Agrippina brought to Claudius as her dowry may be represented by the so-called *Gemma Claudia* (figure 14). This Claudian masterpiece has the emperor and his wife facing Germanicus and Agrippina, with an eagle in the middle and military trophies at the base of the effigies. Agrippina the Younger here embodies the link that connects Germanicus to Claudius and endows the emperor with all the popularity that Germanicus' family had always attracted.[116]

But Claudius made sure that respect for his new wife's family legacy reached an even larger section of the populace. On a sestertius (figure 19) Agrippina the Younger is portrayed on the obverse with a legend highlighting her descent from Germanicus. She was also present in the arch over the via Lata in Rome where her father's statue was placed. There she was called 'Iulia Augusta' and described as daughter of Germanicus, while a young Nero stood by her side.[117]

Agrippina the Younger nevertheless made sure to use the family connections to bolster her status on her own terms too. When Caractacus, leader of the Britons, was brought to Rome in chains to be presented to Claudius, Agrippina was present too – an extraordinary event in the eyes of our sources.[118] She appeared in a gold-threaded military cloak and she sat before the military standards of the Roman cohorts (probably the praetorians) – behaviour that would have been deemed unsuitable for a woman.[119] The recalling of her own mother's feats on the Rhine is here evident (see Chapter 2.3) and after all, stressing the military connection and implying the support of loyal troops was a central characteristic of the 'Julian' faction's ideology which Agrippina had inherited.

We have already pointed out the favour that Nero enjoyed because of his lineage from Germanicus. That he owed this to his mother, however, is something he was not allowed to forget. When Nero was considering killing his own mother in 59 CE, Burrus, the praetorian prefect at the time, reminded the young emperor that 'the praetorians, too devout to the house of the Caesars and to Germanicus' memory, would not have dared to act against his offspring.'[120] This did not deter Nero: Agrippina the Younger was disposed of by a trusted servant of the young *princeps*, paying the price for her 'arrogance and pride' – those same characteristics which had previously doomed her own mother.

Nero did not need to make use of Germanicus' image, unlike his two predecessors. Through his mother, he could claim direct descent from the Divus Augustus, and indeed his legacy of artefacts is full of Augustan symbols.[121] His ideology of power, however, was nothing like Augustus'; indeed, Nero inherited that conception of divine monarchy that his grandmother Agrippina, his uncle Caligula and his own mother had all supported.[122] This proved too much for the conservative Roman senators; with military revolts and disaffection erupting both in and outside Rome, the young Nero was driven to kill himself, bringing to an end Germanicus' line and, with it, the political experience and the existence of the Julio-Claudian family.

Conclusion

To sum up, to what extent could we call someone like Germanicus unlucky then? And what are our reasons for saying so?

Undeniably, Germanicus was unlucky in the simple fact that he died so young. But to what was this sudden and apparently suspicious death due? It should by now be clear that Tiberius had nothing to do with it, contrary to what our literary sources insinuate. It is also very unlikely that the matriarch Livia – beyond some natural affection, the extent of which we cannot verify – would have harmed an individual who played (and would have continued to play) such a key role in the family politics and the stability of the state.

The Senate could not find any evidence for Piso acting on his own to dispose of his rival, let alone that he had been ordered by Tiberius to do so. It is evident, however, that some ill-feeling did exist between the old senator and the young prince. This may have stemmed from the fact that Germanicus had implicitly been tasked by his uncle to keep an eye on the old man, whose appointment was made in order to reconcile him to the new political reality. Germanicus was definitely unlucky to have had Piso as governor of Syria while he was in the east, notwithstanding all the political reasons and machinations which could have been behind such a choice.

Piso's wife Plancina might have acted of her own accord to poison Germanicus, perhaps to spite her long-term rival Agrippina. However, evidence for this is at best sketchy and even Tacitus, the most authoritative of our literary sources, admits that Germanicus' death had been the subject of rumours ever since it occurred.[1] Much more probable is the idea that Germanicus simply died of natural causes. Historian Ronald Syme has demonstrated how unusually high the rate of young noblemen dying in those years was; he suggests that a severe epidemic of some kind may have been circulating at the time and could have been the cause of many premature deaths, including that of Drusus the Younger in 23 CE.[2]

If that was the case, however, why do the literary sources place so much stress on the story of the prince's murder? Did Germanicus truly believe himself to have been poisoned, as the ancient authors report? The second reason for Germanicus to be considered unlucky is related to the answer. It is connected with the way in which others exploited his image and memory, especially after his death. Let us remind ourselves of the potential existence of a pro-Germanicus and anti-Tiberius source contemporary to the events, who may have been part of the young prince's circle and who was used by later historians to inform their works. Because of this possibility, it is paradoxically very difficult to find the 'real' voice of Germanicus in our sources. His political views can be mainly pieced together by integrating the literary accounts with non-literary sources (although we should not forget that even the latter were commissioned and produced following specific orders and intentions). Despite all this, it is quite safe to say that Germanicus probably shared his uncle's view of empire: a rule based on traditionalism and compromise with Rome's upper classes, in line with the Augustan model.

This latter option is not, however, what his wife had in mind for him or for their offspring. And this is where Germanicus was unlucky for a third time: in having a wife (and friends) so devoted to him, yet at the same time wedded to their cause. In order to pursue their goals, Agrippina and her circle did not hesitate to make use of Germanicus' deeds and popularity with the troops to denigrate the emperor Tiberius, eventually even trying to displace him. We have seen to what a destructive end this led them; and yet, Germanicus' memory endured, to be exploited in turn by his son Caligula, his brother Claudius, and his last living daughter, Agrippina the Younger. All these individuals used Germanicus' image and his family link with the Divus Augustus to boost their newly acquired legitimacy to rule Rome.

In the use of his image, could certain traits of Germanicus' character have been altered to achieve the desired effect? The literary sources love stressing his military skills, for instance. And yet, reading between the lines, the picture which emerges is rather different: the young prince comes across as a competent commander, for sure, but he surely was not comparable to extraordinary generals like Alexander the Great or Julius Caesar. Can we consider Germanicus unlucky for this factor too? Perhaps. Still, that he was popular among his soldiers cannot be denied; there is even an instance of his memory lingering among the troops of Syria two hundred years after his death.[3]

Finally, Germanicus was unlucky because after his death the memory of his life was overtaken by *rumores* and exploitation, perhaps the most vicious form of legacy. I would like to conclude the tale of this young man's life with the warning that even Tacitus, always the skilful manipulator, felt compelled to give his reader when relating these events: 'There is always much uncertainty even in events of the greatest importance, for there is always someone who takes for granted any hearsay, regardless of its source, while others change truth into falsehood; both errors then spread, increased and deformed with the passing of time.'[4]

Notes

Introduction

1. Powell, 2016; Rivière, 2016.
2. We use *princeps* in this book as an interchangeable word for 'emperor' and 'ruler', for ease of reading. More details on the terminology are given later in this section.
3. Questa, 2010, p. LII.
4. Feldherr, 2009, p. 175.
5. Edwards, 2011, pp. 1048–9.
6. See for instance, Pelling, 1993; Williams, 2009.
7. Cochran, 1980, p. 193; Lanciotti, 2009, p. 6.
8. *Ibid.*, pp. 8–9.
9. *Ibid.*, p. 12.
10. Cochran, 1980, p. 190.
11. Sordi, 1999, p. 22.
12. Lange and Madsen, 2016, p. 3; Sordi, 1999, p. 11.
13. *Ibid.*, pp. 7–9. Sordi identifies this source as the senator Servilius Nonianus.
14. Cf. Millar, 1964, for this idea.
15. Lange and Madsen, 2016, p. 2.
16. Schulz, 2016.
17. Cf. Starr, 1981.
18. This term refers to those who became senators but were not descendants of the traditional aristocracy.
19. Balmaceda, 2014, p. 340.
20. Cf. Sumner, 1970; Syme, 1978.
21. Cf. Starr, 1981.
22. Cogitore, 2009, p. 51.
23. Balmaceda, 2014.
24. Van Henten, 2018, p. 128.
25. Goud, 1996, p. 479; Nichols, 1975, p. 55.
26. Every reference for this section can be found in the exhaustive, recent works of Lindsay Powell (2016) and Yann Rivière (2016), which discuss Germanicus' early years in depth.

27. For Claudius' physical impairments see Levick, 1999.
28. The Julio-Claudian genealogical tree can be quite the challenge when it comes to names. In this case, there are three 'Drusus' that we need to distinguish. In this book, we will call Germanicus' father Drusus 'the Elder' and Germanicus' stepbrother (Tiberius' son) Drusus 'the Younger'. The second eldest son of Germanicus will be here identified as Drusus 'Caesar'. When the text reads Drusus only, we usually mean Drusus 'the Younger'.
29. This term, from which our word 'emperor' comes from, was originally intended as a military title meaning 'leader' or 'commander'.

Chapter 1

1. Cassius Dio, *Roman History*, 57, 18, 6; *Senatus Consultum de Cn. Pisone patre*, lines 57–8; Suetonius, *Life of Caligula*, 5–6; Tacitus, *Annals*, 2, 72, 2.
2. Braccesi, 2015, pp. 146 ff.
3. Cf. Cresci Marrone, 1978.
4. Tacitus, *Annals*, 2, 72, 2.
5. Suetonius, *Life of Caligula*, 3.
6. The heir presumptive was known as 'Caesar', whereas the reigning emperor took the title of 'Augustus', after the first emperor who bore it.
7. Cassius Dio, *Roman History*, 57, 18, 6–8.
8. Cf. Yavetz, 1999, pp. 28–9. It is interesting to notice that Yavetz tends to scale down the leadership skills of Germanicus, highlighting his averageness in the field, in contrast with his illustrious Macedonian predecessor.
9. Suetonius, *Life of Tiberius*, 15; Tacitus, *Annals*, 1, 3, 5.
10. *Ibid.*, 2, 43, 6. See more on this in Chapter 4.1.
11. *Ibid.*, 2, 53, 1. Tiberius behaved in similar fashion when escorting the ashes of his brother Drusus the Elder back from Germany.
12. *Ibid.*, 4, 4, 1.
13. *Senatus consultum de Cn. Pisone patre*, lines 28–9.
14. Suetonius, *Life of Caligula*, 1; cf. Cassius Dio, *Roman History*, 57, 18, 9; Josephus, *Jewish War*, 18, 54; *Jewish Antiquities*, 54; Pliny the Elder, *Naturalis Historia*, 11, 187.
15. Suetonius, *Life of Tiberius*, 52. These are the notorious *secreta mandata* (secret instructions) of Tiberius to Piso.
16. Tacitus, *Annals*, 2, 73, 5.
17. *Ibid.*, 2, 69, 4 – 71, 3.
18. *Senatus consultum de Cn. Pisone patre*, lines 28–9.
19. Tacitus, *Annals*, 2, 73, 6.

20. Cf. Pani, 1987, pp. 16 ff; Gallotta, 1987, pp. 168 ff. Historian Bruno Gallotta even mentions the existence of a third tradition, originating from the closeness between the old republican aristocracy and Agrippina's followers, in coalition against the imperial family (a coalition which, nonetheless, endured only until Germanicus' death or until 23 CE at the latest, the time of Drusus the Younger's death).
21. Cf. Gallotta, 1987, pp. 195–200.
22. Cf. Syme, 1981, for the high probability of Germanicus' death from natural causes. This latter point is discussed in more depth in the conclusion of this book.
23. Tacitus, *Annals*, 2, 43, 4.
24. *Ibid.*, 2, 75, 1.
25. *Ibid.*, 3, 2, 3.
26. *Ibid.*, 3, 3.
27. Cf. Braccesi, 2015, p. 189; Gallotta, 1987, p. 202.
28. Josephus, *Jewish Antiquities*, 18, 181–2.
29. Shotter, 2000, p. 348.
30. Tacitus, *Annals*, 4, 8, 2.
31. Cassius Dio, *Roman History*, 57, 22, 3.
32. *Ibid.*, 57, 14, 6.
33. *Ibid.*, 58, 2; Tacitus, *Annals*, 5, 2, 1.
34. Cassius Dio, *Roman History*, 58, 21, 1–2.
35. *Senatus consultum de Cn. Pisone patre*, lines 147–50.
36. Cf. Cassius Dio, *Roman History*, 57, 21, 3; Suetonius, *Life of Tiberius*, 32.
37. Cf. Severy, 2000.
38. Ovid, *Letters from Pontus*, 2, 2, lines 69–74.
39. *Ibid.*, 4, 9, lines 105–12.
40. Fraschetti, 1988, pp. 888–9.
41. Tacitus, *Annals*, 3, 5.
42. *Ibid.*, 3, 6.
43. Suetonius, *Life of Caligula*, 6; cf. Fraschetti 1988, p. 885. The *Fasti Ostienses* record 8 December (*VI Idus Decembris*) as the day of public mourning for Germanicus' death.
44. Cf. Potter, 1987, p. 274. According to him, Germanicus' three arches were intended to celebrate his activity from one end of the empire to the other.
45. Germanicus translated from Greek to Latin, and subsequently edited, a very famous Hellenistic astrological poem: the *Phaenomena* of Aratus.
46. Tacitus, *Annals*, 2, 83.

47. González, 1999, p. 125.
48. Cf. Cassius Dio, *Roman History*, 53, 1–3.
49. Cf. Severy, 2000, p. 323.
50. Lebek, 1993, p. 77.
51. Severy, 2000, p. 324.
52. *Tabula Siarensis*, 2, lines 22–4.
53. Severy, 2000, p. 326.
54. *Tabula Siarensis*, 2, lines 18–19.
55. Cf. Gonzalez, 1999, pp. 128 ff.

Chapter 2

1. Tacitus, *Annals*, 1, 3, 5; Velleius Paterculus, *Roman History*, 2, 123, 1.
2. Cassius Dio, *Roman History*, 57, 5, 1; Suetonius, *Life of Tiberius*, 25; Tacitus, *Annals*, 1, 31, 1; Velleius Paterculus, *Roman History*, 2, 125, 1.
3. Sordi, 1999, p. 493; Syme, 1958, pp. 364–6. Cf. Introduction.
4. Tacitus, *Annals*, 1, 14, 3.
5. Cassius Dio, *Roman History*, 57, 6, 2; Suetonius, *Life of Tiberius*, 25; Tacitus, *Annals*, 1, 35, 4; 42–3.
6. Tacitus, *Annals*, 1, 7, 6; cf. Cassius Dio, *Roman History*, 57, 3, 1; 4, 1; 6, 2.
7. Tacitus, *Annals*, 1, 35, 4–5. Cf. Cassius Dio, *Roman History*, 57, 5, 2; Gallotta, 1987, pp. 78 ff.; Yavetz, 1999, pp. 18–19.
8. Tacitus, *Annals*, 1, 39, 3.
9. *Ibid.*, 1, 40–1; cf. Cassius Dio, *Roman History*, 57, 5, 6–7.
10. Tacitus, *Annals*, 1, 49, 2.
11. The fact that the army provided the key to imperial power emerged on many occasions at critical moments of the empire's history, such as the civil war of 68–9 CE and the so-called 'military anarchy' of the third century CE.
12. Velleius Paterculus, *Roman History*, 2, 125.
13. Tacitus, *Annals*, 1, 42–3.
14. *Ibid.*, 1, 36, 3; cf. Cassius Dio, *Roman History*, 57, 5, 3.
15. Tacitus, *Annals*, 1, 49, 3.
16. *Ibid.*, 1, 52, 1.
17. *Ibid.*, 1, 60, 3; cf. Cassius Dio, *Roman History*, 57, 18, 1. For the second eagle see Tacitus, *Annals*, 2, 25, 1–2.
18. *Ibid.*, 1, 61, 1.
19. Braccesi, 1987, pp. 57–8.
20. Tacitus, *Annals*, 1, 62, 2; cf. Cassius Dio, *Roman History*, 57, 18, 1; Suetonius, *Life of Caligula*, 3.
21. For the meaning of the word *imperator* see note 29 of the Introduction.

22. Gallotta, 1987, pp. 123 ff. To confirm his hypothesis, Gallotta proposes to see Germanicus' acclamation as *imperator* in 15 CE as a way to strengthen consensus towards him; Tiberius would have allowed his nephew this in order to reinforce Germanicus' position. In 16 CE, after the military operations had come back under the *auspicia* of Tiberius, it was only fair that it should be he (as per custom, the main augur at that point) and not Germanicus, who would be acclaimed *imperator* by the soldiers.
23. Tacitus, *Annals*, 2, 5–6.
24. Cf. Cresci Marrone, 1978, pp. 210–11.
25. Tacitus, *Annals*, 2, 16, 1.
26. The detailed narration of the battle of Idistavisus can be found in Tacitus, *Annals*, 2, 17.
27. See Tacitus, *Annals*, 2, 19–21, for the events at the 'Vallum of the Angrivarii'.
28. Tacitus, *Annals*, 2, 22, 1. According to Cassius Dio (*Roman History*, 56, 25, 2), Germanicus was already present on the Rhine under Tiberius' command around 10/11 CE. Unfortunately, we have no specific details about Germanicus' involvement in these campaigns. For a discussion see Powell, 2016; Rivière, 2016.
29. Tacitus, *Annals*, 2, 26, 4–5.
30. Velleius Paterculus, *Roman History*, 2, 97, 4; 105–9; 120–1.
31. *Ibid.*, 2, 120, 1.
32. Roberto, 2020, p.21.
33. Velleius Paterculus, *Roman History*, 2, 121, 1–2.
34. *Tabula Siarensis*, 1, lines 12–18.
35. Suetonius, *Life of Tiberius*, 37; Tacitus, *Annals*, 2, 26, 2; Velleius Paterculus, *Roman History*, 2, 109, 1.
36. Tacitus, *Annals*, 2, 26, 4.
37. Gallotta, 1987, p. 133.
38. Tacitus, *Annals*, 2, 1–4.
39. Powell, 2023, pp. 389 ff.
40. Levick, 1972; 1999, pp. 35 ff. Allegedly, Tiberius' departure was intended to clear the way for Augustus' young heirs, Gaius Caesar and Lucius Caesar, although a breakdown in his relationship with Julia, Augustus' daughter and mother of the boys (and at this point his wife) cannot be entirely dismissed.
41. Suetonius, *Life of Divus Augustus*, 64.
42. Cassius Dio, *Roman History*, 55, 10, 20–1; Velleius Paterculus, *Roman History*, 2, 101, 1.
43. Velleius Paterculus, *Roman History*, 2, 101, 2–3.
44. Cassius Dio, *Roman History*, 55, 10a, 5.

45. Velleius Paterculus, *Roman History*, 2, 102, 2–3.
46. Low, 2016, pp. 228–9; 234. Cf. Luttwak, 1979, for a deep analysis of the Julio-Claudian emperors' relationship with their client-states in the east.
47. Cf. Montanari Caldini, 1987, pp. 153–71, for Germanicus' astronomical interests. Cf. Giancarlo, 2010, for Germanicus' surviving epigrams.
48. Tacitus, *Annals*, 2, 60–1. All the following quotations are to be referred to these two chapters. Cf. Capponi, 2020, p. 126; Cresci Marrone, 1978, pp. 211 ff.
49. The statue was 'silenced' during the reign of Septimius Severus, around 200 CE, when another earthquake moved its stones again and the cavity was blocked. Cf. Pliny the Elder, *Naturalis Historia*, 36, 7; 11; 58.
50. Similar events during Germanicus' eastern journey should be read by adopting the same key, that is, visits to places which aroused the young man's interest in anything 'antiquarian' and mystical. Such places were Actium, the site of the ultimate battle between Germanicus' ancestors, Augustus and Mark Antony; Troy, the mythical birthplace of the *gens Iulia*, from whom Germanicus partly descended; and the oracle of Apollo Clarus at Colophon, in modern-day western Turkey. Germanicus would have liked to stop at the island of Samothrace as well, to participate in the mysteries there, but he was blown back by contrary winds and unable to land.
51. Tacitus, *Annals*, 2, 59, 2.
52. Suetonius, *Life of Tiberius*, 52.
53. Cf. Gallotta, 1987, pp. 187–8.
54. Tacitus, *Annals*, 2, 43, 1; Velleius Paterculus, *Roman History*, 2, 129.
55. *Senatus consultum de Cn. Pisone patre*, lines 34–6.
56. Josephus, *Jewish Antiquities*, 15, 350–51.
57. The official nomenclature of the document is *Papyrus Oxyrhynchus XXV 2435*. See Lobel and Turner, 1959, pp. 102 ff.
58. *Papyrus Oxhyrynchus XXV 2435*, line 9.
59. Tacitus, *Annals*, 2, 59–60; cf. Josephus, *Against Apion*, 2, 63; Suetonius, *Life of Tiberius*, 52.
60. Capponi, 2020, p. 128.
61. *Papyrus Oxyrhynchus XXV 2435*, lines 16–21.
62. See, for instance, two inscriptions from Myra in Lycia (*IGRRP III 720–1*), dated 29 CE, where Tiberius and his mother Livia are addressed as god and goddess respectively.
63. Cf. Gallotta, 1987, p. 159.
64. Seager, 1972, p. 104.
65. Capponi, 2020, p. 131.

66. Suetonius, *Life of Tiberius*, 52.
67. Suetonius, *Life of Divus Titus*, 5.
68. Tacitus, *Annals*, 2, 59, 2.
69. *Ibid.*, 2, 53, 3.
70. *Ibid.*, 2, 57, 4.
71. Gallotta, 1987, p. 162.
72. Josephus, *Jewish Antiquities*, 16, 2, 1.
73. Tacitus, *Annals*, 2, 56.
74. *Senatus consultum de Cn. Pisone patre*, lines 43–4.
75. For the dynastic message behind this statuary group see Chapter 4.1.
76. Suetonius, *Life of Tiberius*, 11; 13.
77. Tacitus, *Annals*, 1, 33, 3. Cf. Dennison, 2010.
78. For this and above, see Rohr Vio, 2011, pp. 85–8.
79. Cf. Rohr Vio, 2011, p. 88.
80. *Ibid.*, p. 89.
81. Pani, 2003, p. 38.
82. Velleius Paterculus, *Roman History*, 2, 100, 5.
83. Cf., for instance, Syme, 1939, p. 282.
84. Cf. Braccesi, 2012, pp. 115 ff.; Pani, 2003, p. 38; Rohr Vio, 2011, pp. 90–1.
85. Rohr Vio, 2011, pp. 94–6.
86. Pani, 2003, p. 39.
87. *Ibid.*, p. 40.
88. *Ibid.*, pp. 41–3. For a discussion of Germanicus and Agrippina's circle of friends, see Pani, 1968.
89. Pani, 2003, p. 64.
90. Tacitus, *Annals*, 2, 72, 1.
91. *Ibid.*, 1, 41, 2.
92. Suetonius, *Life of Caligula*, 9.
93. Tacitus, *Annals*, 1, 69.
94. Not every scholar agrees with this interpretation. Cf. Cenerini, 2020, p. 142, who prefers reading Agrippina's major involvement on the Rhine as a later, anachronistic reinterpretation of the role of an imperial woman, much more akin to the behaviours of second-century imperial women.
95. Cf. Braccesi, 2015, pp. 54 ff.; Gallotta, 1987, pp. 57–64; Seager, 1972, pp. 89–93; Storoni Mazzolani, 1981, p. 147; Valentini, 2014.
96. For Libo's family connections see Weinrib, 1968.
97. Tacitus, *Annals*, 2, 27. Cf. Cassius Dio, *Roman History*, 57, 15, 4–6; Suetonius, *Life of Tiberius*, 25; Velleius Paterculus, *Roman History*, 2, 129.

98. Cf. Shotter, 1972, pp. 92–3.
99. Even Tacitus, for once, believes that the emperor's conduct in doing so is not malicious.
100. Tacitus, *Annals*, 2, 32, 3.
101. Cf. Valentini, 2014.
102. Cassius Dio, *Roman History*, 57, 16; Suetonius, *Life of Tiberius*, 25; Tacitus, *Annals*, 2, 39, 1–2.
103. Tacitus, *Annals*, 1, 6.
104. For a comprehensive analysis of the various interpretations of the mysterious death of Agrippa Postumus see Detweiler, 1970.
105. Tacitus, *Annals*, 1, 53, 2.
106. Suetonius, *Life of Divus Augustus*, 19. Cf. Sordi, 2002, p. 321.
107. Tacitus, *Annals*, 2, 39, 2–3.
108. Cassius Dio, *Roman History*, 57, 16, 3–4.
109. Tacitus, *Annals*, 2, 40, 3.
110. Cf. Levick, 1999, pp. 118–19; Rohr Vio, 2000, pp. 266–9; Sordi, 2002, pp. 316–17. Pettinger, 2012, clearly links Clemens' insurrection and Libo's failed 'conspiracy' to the same mastermind.
111. Tacitus, *Annals*, 4, 52, 2.

Chapter 3

1. Tacitus, *Annals*, 2, 43, 4.
2. Velleius Paterculus, *Roman History*, 2, 130, 3.
3. Cooley, 1998, p. 203; Syme, 1939, pp. 334–5.
4. Cooley, 1998, p. 204. Cf. *senatus consultum de Cn. Pisone patre*, lines 26–7, where Piso's 'savagery' is opposed to Germanicus' restraint and forbearance.
5. Tacitus, *Annals*, 2, 43, 2.
6. *Ibid.*, 2, 43, 3.
7. Cassius Dio, *Roman History*, 57, 15, 9.
8. Tacitus, *Annals*, 1, 74, 1–6.
9. Suetonius, *Life of Caligula*, 2.
10. Drogula, 2015, p. 137.
11. Pani, 2003, p. 43.
12. Syme, 1939, p. 368.
13. Tacitus, *Annals*, 3, 12, 1. Cf. *senatus consultum de Cn. Pisone patre*, lines 30-32.
14. Braccesi, 2015, pp. 91-2; Pani, 1987, p. 2.
15. Syme, 1939, p. 368.
16. Drogula, 2015.
17. *Ibid.*, p. 128.
18. Traina and Buongiorno, 2020, p. 107.

19. Tacitus, *Annals*, 2, 55.
20. *Ibid.*, 2, 57.
21. Cf. Gallotta, 1987, p. 157.
22. Traina and Buongiorno, 2020, p. 110.
23. Tacitus, *Annals*, 2, 57, 2.
24. Mercogliano, 2009, pp. 33–6.
25. *Ibid.*, pp. 56 ff.
26. For all the Parthian matters, see Tacitus, *Annals*, 2, 2–4.
27. Tacitus, *Annals*, 2, 58, 1.
28. *Senatus consultum de Cn. Pisone patre*, line 44.
29. Tacitus, *Annals*, 2, 69, 1.
30. *Ibid.*, 2, 69, 3.
31. Cf. Drogula, 2015, p. 135, for what renouncing someone's friendship meant.
32. *Senatus consultum de Cn. Pisone patre*, lines 28–9.
33. Tacitus, *Annals*, 2, 70, 2.
34. *Senatus consultum de Cn. Pisone patre*, lines 5–6; Tacitus, *Annals*, 3, 10, 3.
35. Tacitus, *Annals*, 3, 12.
36. *Ibid.*, 2, 74, 2.
37. *Ibid.*, 3, 7, 2.
38. *Ibid.*, 3, 12, 7.
39. *Ibid.*, 3, 14, 3.
40. *Senatus consultum de Cn. Pisone patre*, line 5.
41. Tacitus, *Annals*, 3, 14, 1.
42. *Senatus consultum de Cn. Pisone patre*, lines 26–8.
43. *Ibid.*, lines 37–40.
44. *Ibid*, lines 52 ff.
45. *Ibid.*, lines 45–50; Tacitus, *Annals*, 2, 14, 2.
46. Tacitus, *Annals*, 2, 77, 3.
47. *Ibid.*, 2, 76, 2.
48. *Ibid.*, 3, 80, 2.
49. *Ibid.*, 3, 15, 2.
50. *Ibid.*, 3, 15, 3. Cf. Cassius Dio, *Roman History*, 57, 18, 10.
51. See, for instance, Braccesi, 2015, pp. 167–8.
52. For all the dispositions taken against Piso after his death see the *senatus consultum de Cn. Pisone patre*, lines 71–108.
53. Bodel, 1999, p. 59.
54. Cooley, 1998, pp. 200–1. Cf Severy, 2000, p. 327.
55. *Senatus consultum de Cn. Pisone patre*, lines 33–4.
56. Tacitus, *Annals*, 2, 43, 5.
57. Cf. Dennison, 2010.

58. Tacitus, *Annals*, 2, 55, 6.
59. Valerius Maximus, *Nine books of memorable deeds and sayings*, 5, 3.
60. Tacitus, *Annals*, 2, 82, 2.
61. *Ibid.*, 2, 75, 1; 3, 4, 2.
62. *Ibid.*, 3, 15, 1.
63. *Senatus consultum de Cn. Pisone patre*, line 113.
64. Tacitus, *Annals*, 3, 16, 4.
65. Cf. Braccesi, 2015.
66. Tacitus, *Annals*, 3, 17, 1. Cf. *senatus consultum de Cn. Pisone patre*, lines 115–20.
67. *Ibid.*, 2, 34, 2–4.
68. See Chapter 1.2 for this.
69. Severy, 2000, p. 331.
70. *Ibid.*, p. 334.
71. Tacitus, *Annals*, 3, 17, 2.
72. *Ibid.*, 3, 18, 1.
73. Cassius Dio, *Roman History*, 58, 22, 5.
74. Tacitus, *Annals*, 6, 26, 3.

Chapter 4

1. Tacitus, *Annals*, 2, 26, 4.
2. Suetonius, *Life of Tiberius*, 52.
3. Hurlet, 1997.
4. Levick, 1966.
5. *Ibid.*, pp. 239–40.
6. Angeli Bertinelli, 1987, p. 39.
7. *Senatus consultum de Cn. Pisone patre*, lines 125–30.
8. Ovid, *Tristia*, 4, 2, lines 9–10.
9. Ovid, *Letters from Pontus*, 4, 9, lines 105–12.
10. De Maria, 1988, pp. 276–7.
11. Lebek, 1989.
12. Lanciani, 1990, p. 227.
13. Traina and Buongiorno, 2020, p. 117.
14. Giuliani, 2010, pp. 11–30. Not every scholar agrees with this interpretation, however. For instance, Traina and Buongiorno (2020, pp. 115–16) identify the figure on Augustus' left side not as Drusus the Younger but as Drusus the Elder, Germanicus' father.
15. Saladino, 1980, pp. 234–5.
16. De Maria, 1988, p. 328.
17. *CIL XIII 1036*.
18. *Année Epigraphique*, 1993, n. 204.
19. *IGRRP IV 1549*.

20. Grassigli, 2020, pp. 200–1.
21. *ILS 6896.*
22. Piattelli, 1987, p. 89.
23. Suspène, 2013, p.187.
24. Tacitus, *Annals*, 2, 43, 6.
25. *Ibid.*, 2, 53, 1.
26. *Ibid.*, 2, 71, 1; 3, 2, 3.
27. *Tabula Siarensis*, 2, lines 18–19.
28. Tacitus, *Annals*, 4, 4, 1.
29. Bird, 1969, pp. 61–2.
30. Cenerini, 2014, p.130.
31. Pani, 2003, pp. 44–5.
32. Tacitus, *Annals*, 3, 56, 1; 4.
33. *Ibid.*, 2, 84.
34. Gallotta, 1987, pp. 200–1.
35. Cassius Dio, *Roman History*, 57, 19, 7.
36. Velleius Paterculus, *Roman History*, 2, 126, 3.
37. Bird, 1969, p. 65; Cenerini, 2014, p. 129.
38. Cassius Dio, *Roman History*, 57, 22; Pliny the Elder, *Naturalis Historia*, 29, 20; Suetonius, *Life of Tiberius*, 62; Tacitus, *Annals*, 4, 3–5.
39. Cenerini, 2014, p.128; Hurlet, 1997, p. 223; Levick, 1999, p. 127.
40. Cf. Seager, 1972, pp. 180–1.
41. Tacitus, *Annals*, 4, 39; cf. Cenerini, 2014, p.129.
42. Tacitus, *Annals*, 4, 40, 2.
43. Cenerini, 2020, p. 144.
44. Tacitus, *Annals*, 4, 40, 3.
45. Cenerini, 2020, p. 148.
46. Tacitus, *Annals*, 4, 8, 4–5. Cf. Suetonius, *Life of Tiberius*, 54.
47. Giuliani, 2010; Traina and Buongiorno, 2020.
48. *CIL X 6101.*
49. Rogers, 1931, p. 141.
50. Bird, 1969, p. 71; Shotter, 1967, p. 713.
51. Shotter, 2000, p. 349.
52. Tacitus, *Annals*, 3, 49, 1. Cf. Cassius Dio, *Roman History*, 57, 20, 3–4.
53. Shotter, 1969, pp.16–17.
54. Tacitus, *Annals*, 4, 18, 1; 19, 1.
55. Shotter, 1967, p. 216.
56. Tacitus, *Annals*, 4, 28–9.
57. *Ibid.*, 4, 31, 3; 52, 1.
58. *Ibid.*, 5, 8, 1.
59. *Ibid.*, 4, 15, 3.

60. Braccesi, 2015, p. 176.
61. Tacitus, *Annals*, 4, 53, 1.
62. *Ibid.*, 4, 17, 1–3. Cf. Suetonius, *Life of Tiberius*, 53.
63. Cassius Dio, *Roman History*, 58, 23, 1.
64. Tacitus, *Annals*, 4, 52, 1-3. Cf. Suetonius, *Life of Tiberius*, 53.
65. Tacitus, *Annals*, 4, 53, 2.
66. For the first theory, see Braccesi, 2015, p. 187; for the second, cf. Cenerini, 2020, p. 148.
67. Tacitus, *Annals*, 4, 54; cf. Suetonius, *Life of Tiberius*, 53.
68. Cf. Introduction, p. X, in relation to Tacitus' narrative intentions in describing Tiberius' withdrawal to Capri.
69. Suetonius, *Life of Tiberius*, 10.
70. Deline, 2015, pp. 766–72.
71. Tacitus, *Annals*, 5, 3, 2–3.
72. Velleius Paterculus, *Roman History*, 2, 130, 4.
73. Tacitus, *Annals*, 4, 60, 1.
74. *Ibid.*, 4, 60, 2.
75. Suetonius, *Life of Tiberius*, 53.
76. Cassius Dio, *Roman History*, 58, 3, 8.
77. Suetonius, *Life of Tiberius*, 54; *Life of Caligula*, 7.
78. Cassius Dio, *Roman History*, 58, 8, 1–2.
79. Suetonius, *Life of Tiberius*, 61.
80. Nichols, 1975.
81. Cf. for instance, Boddington, 1963; Pani, 2003, pp. 44–5.
82. Suetonius, *Life of Tiberius*, 54.
83. *Ibid.*, 53–4; Tacitus, *Annals*, 6, 23, 2; 25, 1.
84. Tuplin, 1987, p. 790.
85. Shotter, 2000, p. 355.
86. Cassius Dio, *Roman History*, 58, 25, 1; Tacitus, *Annals*, 5, 10.
87. Cassius Dio, *Roman History*, 59, 8; Suetonius, *Life of Caligula*, 23.
88. Cassius Dio, *Roman History*, 59, 3, 8.
89. Cristofoli, 2020, p. 161.
90. Suetonius, *Life of Caligula*, 13. Cf. Tacitus, *Annals*, 6, 46, 1.
91. Josephus, *Jewish Antiquities*, 18, 205–10.
92. For instance, David Shotter (2000, p. 357) sees Agrippina as the inspiration for Caligula's future political views, whereas Mario Pani (2003, pp. 46; 66–7) argues that the emperor's views stemmed from his time in the household of Antonia.
93. Suetonius, *Life of Caligula*, 14.
94. *Ibid.*, 15.
95. Levick, 1999, p. 152. Cf. Barrett, 1989, p. 125.
96. Grassigli, 2020, p. 190.

97. The coin is classified as *RIC I Gaius 57* in the *Roman Imperial Coinage* series. All the coins here described, unless differently specified, were commissioned by the central government, and not by provincial mints.
98. Suspène, 2013, p. 179.
99. Panvini Rosati, 1987, p.83.
100. Piattelli, 1987, p. 88.
101. Suspène, 2013, p. 178.
102. For the controversial narration of Claudius' accession to the throne, see Cassius Dio, *Roman History*, 60, 1; Josephus, *Jewish Antiquities*, 19, 162 ff.; Suetonius, *Life of Claudius*, 10.
103. Galimberti, 2020, p. 180.
104. Josephus, *Jewish Antiquities*, 19, 223.
105. Cf. Levick, 1999, pp. 11–28.
106. Tacitus, *Annals*, 3, 18, 3–4.
107. *CIL VI 920.*
108. *Ibid., 924.*
109. Cf. Levick, 1999, p. 143.
110. *Ibid.*, p. 183.
111. *Ibid.*, p. 45.
112. Suspène, 2013, p.182.
113. Levick, 1999, pp. 159–61.
114. Tacitus, *Annals*, 12, 2, 3.
115. *Ibid.*, 11, 12, 1.
116. Cenerini, 2020, p. 150.
117. Cf. Barrett, 1996, p. 117.
118. For the sources' astonishment at such behaviours, cf. Chapters 1.2 and 3.4.
119. Cassius Dio, *Roman History*, 60, 33, 7; Tacitus, *Annals*, 12, 37, 5–6.
120. *Ibid.*, 14, 7, 3-4.
121. Cf. Suspène, 2013, pp. 182–4.
122. Cf. Lazzeretti, 2000.

Conclusion

1. Tacitus, *Annals*, 3, 19, 2.
2. Syme, 1981, pp. 127–8.
3. Angeli Bertinelli, 1987, p. 48. The *Feriale Duranum*, a calendar of religious observances from the garrison city of Dura Europos in Roman Syria, celebrates Germanicus' birthday on 24 May.
4. Tacitus, *Annals*, 3, 19, 2.

Bibliography and Further Reading

Ancient sources

Berlin Papyrus 11547
Cassius Dio, *Roman History*
Josephus, *Against Apion*
Josephus, *Jewish Antiquities*
Josephus, *Jewish War*
Ovid, *Letters from Pontus*
Ovid, *Tristia*
Papyrus Oxyrhynchus XXV 2435
Pliny the Elder, *Naturalis Historia*
Senatus consultum de Cn. Pisone patre
Suetonius, *Life of the Twelve Caesars*
Tabula Hebana
Tabula Siarensis
Tacitus, *Annals*
Valerius Maximus, *Nine books of memorable deeds and sayings*
Velleius Paterculus, *Roman History*

Epigraphic collections

Année Epigraphique
CIL (*Corpus Inscriptionum Latinarum*)
IGRRP (*Inscriptiones Graecae ad Res Romanas Pertinentes*)
ILS (*Inscriptiones Latinae Selectae*)

Numismatic collections

RIC (*Roman Imperial Coinage*)

Modern studies

Akveld, V., *Germanicus* (Gröningen 1961).

Angeli Bertinelli, M., 'Germanico nella documentazione epigrafica', in G. Bonamente and M. Segoloni (eds) *Germanico. La persona, la personalitá, il personaggio* (Rome 1987), pp. 25–51.

Balmaceda, C., 'The Virtues of Tiberius in Velleius' Histories', *Historia: Zeitschrift für Alte Geschichte,* 63, 3 (2014), pp. 340–63.

Barbanera, M. (ed.), *Germanico Cesare a un passo dall'impero* (Perugia 2021).

Barnes, T., 'The Composition of Cassius Dio's *Roman History*', *Phoenix*, 38 (1984), pp. 240–55.

Barnes, T., 'Tacitus and the *Senatus consultum de Cn. Pisone Patre*', *Phoenix*, 52 (1998), pp.125–48.

Barrett, A., *Caligula, the Corruption of Power* (London and New York 1989).

Barrett, A., *Agrippina: Sister of Caligula, Wife of Claudius, Mother of Nero* (London 1996).

Bird, H., 'L. Aelius Seianus and his Political Significance', *Latomus*, 28, 1 (1969), pp. 61–98.

Boddington, A., 'Sejanus: whose conspiracy?', *The American Journal of Philology*, 84, 1 (1963), pp. 1–16.

Bodel, J., 'Punishing Piso', *The American Journal of Philology*, 120, 1 (1999), pp. 43–63.

Borgo, A., 'Velleio Patercolo, Tacito e il Principato di Tiberio: un tentativo di interpretazione in chiave storica', *Vichiana* (1978), pp. 280–95.

Braccesi, L., 'Germanico e l'*imitatio Alexandri* in Occidente', in G. Bonamente and M. Segoloni (eds) *Germanico. La persona, la personalità, il personaggio* (Rome 1987), pp. 53–65.

Braccesi, L., *Giulia, la figlia di Augusto* (Bari 2012).

Braccesi, L., *Agrippina, la sposa di un mito* (Bari 2015).

Buongiorno, P., *Claudio. Il principe inatteso* (Palermo 2017).

Cantineau, J., 'Textes Palmyréniens du temple de Bêl', *Syria*, 12, 2 (1939), pp. 139–41.

Capponi, L., 'Germanico in Egitto tra storia e memoria', in A. Galimberti, R. Cristofoli and F. Rohr Vio (eds) *Germanico nel contesto politico di età Giulio Claudia. La figura, il carisma, la memoria* (Rome 2020), pp. 123–39.

Cenerini, F., *Dive e donne. Mogli, madri, figlie e sorelle degli imperatori romani da Augusto a Commodo* (Imola 2009).

Cenerini, F., '(Claudia) Livia Giulia', *Archimède: Archéologie et histoire ancienne*, 1 (2014), pp. 124–32.

Cenerini, F., 'La figura e la memoria di Germanico nell'azione femminile', in A. Galimberti, R. Cristofoli and F. Rohr Vio (eds) *Germanico nel contesto politico di età Giulio Claudia. La figura, il carisma, la memoria* (Rome 2020), pp. 141–53.

Christ, K., *Drusus und Germanicus: Der Eintritt der Römer in Germanien* (Paderborn 1956).

Cipollone, M., '*Senatus consultum de honoribus Germanici decernendis:* contributo alla lettura della *Tabula Siarensis* da un'iscrizione inedita del museo archeologico di Perugia', *Bollettino di archeologia online. Direzione generale per le antichità*, II, 2–3 (2011), pp. 3–18.

Cochran, L., 'Suetonius' Conception of Imperial Character', *Biography*, 3, 3 (1980), pp. 189–201.

Cogitore, I., 'Les portraits chez Velléius Paterculus', *Latomus*, 68, 1 (2009), pp. 51–72.

Colin, J., 'Les consuls du Cesar-Pharaon Caligula et l'heritage de Germanicus', *Latomus*, 13, 3 (1954), pp. 209–26.

Connal, R., 'Velleius Paterculus: The Soldier and the Senator', *The Classical World*, 107, 1 (2013), pp. 49-62.

Cooley, A., 'The moralizing message of the *senatus consultum de Cn. Pisone patre*', *Greece and Rome,* 45, 2 (1998), pp. 199–212.

Cresci Marrone, G., 'Germanico tra mito d'Alessandro ed *exemplum* d'Augusto', *Sileno,* 4 (1978), pp. 209–26.

Cresci Marrone, G., 'Germanico e l'*imitatio Alexandri* in Oriente', in G. Bonamente and M. Segoloni (eds) *Germanico. La persona, la personalità, il personaggio* (Roma 1987), pp. 67–77.

Cristofoli, R., *Caligola. Una breve vita nella competizione politica (anni 12–41 d.C.)* (Milan 2018).

Cristofoli, R., 'La promozione di Caligola sotto Tiberio: fra mito di Germanico e attualità politica', in A. Galimberti, R. Cristofoli and F. Rohr Vio (eds) *Germanico nel contesto politico di età Giulio Claudia. La figura, il carisma, la memoria* (Rome 2020), pp. 155–74.

Damon, C., 'The Trial of Cn. Piso in Tacitus' *Annals* and the *Senatus consultum de Cn. Pisone patre*: New Light on Narrative Technique', *American Journal of Philology,* 120, 1 (1999), pp. 143–62.

Deline, T., 'The Criminal Charges against Agrippina the Elder in A.D. 27 and 29', *The Classical Quarterly,* 65, 2 (2015), pp. 766–72.

Della Corte, F. and Levi, M., '*Tabula Hebana*', *La parola del passato,* 14 (1950), pp. 98–107.

De Maria, S., *Gli archi onorari di Roma e dell'Italia romana* (Rome 1988).

Dennison, M., *Empress of Rome: The Life of Livia* (London 2010).

Detweiler, R., 1970. 'Historical Perspectives on the Death of Agrippa Postumus', *The Classical Journal*, 65, 7 (1970), pp. 289–95.

Drogula, F., 'Who was watching whom? A reassessment of the conflict between Germanicus and Piso', *The American Journal of Philology,* 136, 1 (2015), pp. 121–53.

Eck, W., Caballos, A. and Fernandez, F., *Das Senatus consultum de Cn. Pisone patre* (Munich 1996).

Edwards, R., 'Tacitus, Tiberius and Capri', *Latomus,* 70, 4 (2011), pp. 1047–57.

Fantham, E., *Julia Augusti, The Emperor's Daughter* (London 2006).

Feldherr, A., 'The Poisoned Chalice: Rumour and Historiography in Tacitus' Account of the Death of Drusus', *Materiali e discussioni per l'analisi dei testi classici,* 61 (2009), pp. 175–89.

Fraschetti, A., 'Morte dei principi ed eroi della famiglia di Augusto', *Annali di archeologia e storia antica. Istituto universitario orientale,* 6 (1984), pp. 151–89.

Fraschetti, A., 'La *Tabula Hebana,* la *Tabula Siarensis* e il *iustitium* per la morte di Germanico', *Mélanges de l'École française de Rome. Antiquité,* 100, 2 (1988), pp. 867–89.

Fraschetti, A., 'L'eroizzazione di Germanico', in A. Fraschetti (ed.) *La commemorazione di Germanico nella documentazione epigrafica* (Rome 2000), pp. 141–62.

Galimberti, A., 'Germanico e Claudio', in A. Galimberti, R. Cristofoli and F. Rohr Vio (eds) *Germanico nel contesto politico di età Giulio Claudia. La figura, il carisma, la memoria* (Rome 2020), pp. 175–85.

Galimberti, A., Cristofoli, R. and Rohr Vio, F. (eds), *Germanico nel contesto politico di età Giulio-Claudia: la figura, il carisma, la memoria* (Rome 2020).

Gallotta, B., *Germanico* (Rome 1987).

Gatti, C., 'Gli *honores* postumi a Germanico nella *Tabula Hebana*', *La parola del passato,* 14 (1950), pp. 151–7.

Giancarlo, B., 'Gli 'epigrammi' di Germanico', *Rivista di cultura classica e medioevale,* 52, 1 (2010), pp. 81–105.

Gissell, J., 'Germanicus as an Alexander Figure', *Classica et Mediaevalia,* 52 (2001), pp. 277–301.

Giua, M., 'Germanico nel racconto tacitiano della rivolta delle legioni renane', *RIL* (1976), pp. 102–13.

Giuliani, L., *Ein Geschenk für den Kaiser: das Geheimnis des grossen Kameo* (Munich 2010).

González, J., 'Tacitus, Germanicus, Piso, and the *Tabula Siarensis*', *The American Journal of Philology,* 20, 1 (1999), pp. 123–42.

Goud, T., 'The Sources of Josephus *Antiquities* 19', *Historia: Zeitschrift für Alte Geschichte,* 45, 4 (1996), pp. 472–82.

Grassigli, G., 'L'immagine di Germanico. Iconografia della speranza e del ricordo', in A. Galimberti, R. Cristofoli and F. Rohr Vio (eds) *Germanico nel contesto politico di età Giulio Claudia. La figura, il carisma, la memoria* (Rome 2020), pp. 187–210.

Gregori, G., 'Una dedica monumentale a Germanico da Piazza Nicosia', *Archeologia Classica,* 45, 1 (1993), pp. 351–65.

Grimal, P., *Tacite* (Paris 1990).

Hennig, D., 'Zur Aegyptenreise des Germanicus', *Chiron: Mitteilungen der Kommission für Alte Geschichte und Epigraphik des Deutschen Archäologischen Instituts,* 2 (1972), pp. 349–65.

Van Henten, J., 'Josephus as Narrator', in E. Becker and J. Rüpke (eds) *Autoren in religiösen literarischen Texten der späthellenistischen und der frühkaiserzeitlichen Welt: Zwölf Fallstudien* (Tübingen 2018), pp. 121–50.

Hurlet, F., *Les collègues du prince sous Auguste et Tibère. De la legalité républicaine à la légitimité dynastique* (Rome 1997).

Hurley, D., 'Gaius Caligula in the Germanicus Tradition', *The American Journal of Philology,* 110, 2 (1989), pp. 316–38.

Kelly, B., 'Tacitus, Germanicus and the kings of Egypt', *The Classical Quarterly,* 60, 1 (2010), pp. 221–37.

Koestermann, E., 'Die Feldzüge des Germanicus, 14–16 n. Chr.', *Historia: Zeitschrift für Alte Geschichte,* 6, 4 (1957), pp. 429–79.

Koestermann, E., 'Die Mission des Germanicus im Orient', *Historia: Zeitschrift für Alte Geschichte,* 7, 3 (1958), pp. 358–71.

Kokkinos, N., *Antonia Augusta: Portrait of a great Roman lady* (London and New York, 1992).

Lanciani, R., *Storia degli scavi di Roma e notizie intorno le collezioni romane di antichità* (Rome 1990).

Lanciotti, S., 'Introduzione', in *Svetonio: Vite dei Cesari* (Milan 2009), pp. 5–14.

Lange, C. and Madsen, J., 'Between History and Politics', in C. Lange and J. Madsen (eds) *Cassius Dio: Greek Intellectual and Roman Politician* (Leiden 2016), pp. 1–10.

Lazzeretti, A., 'Riflessioni sull'opera autobiografica di Agrippina Minore', *Studia Historica, Historia Antigua,* 18 (2000), pp. 177–90.
Lebek, W., 'Die Postumen Ehrenbögen und der Triumph des Drusus Caesar', *Zeitschrift für Papyrologie und Epigraphik,* 78 (1989), pp. 83–91.
Lebek, W., 'Intenzione e composizione della *Rogatio Valeria Aurelia*', *Zeitschrift für Papyrologie und Epigraphik,* 98 (1993), pp. 77–95.
Levi, M., 'L'esclusione dei senatori romani dall'Egitto augusteo', *Aegyptus,* 5 (1924), pp. 231-235.
Levick, B., 'Drusus Caesar and the Adoptions of A.D. 4', *Latomus,* 25 (1966), pp. 227–44.
Levick, B., 'Tiberius' Retirement to Rhodes in 6 BC', *Latomus,* 31, 3 (1972), pp. 779–813.
Levick, B., *Tiberius the Politician* (London and New York 1999).
Levick, B., *Claudius* (London and New York 2001).
Lobel, E. and Turner, E. (eds), *The Oxyrhynchus Papyri,* Part 25 (London 1959).
Low, K., 'Germanicus on tour: history, diplomacy and the promotion of a dynasty', *The Classical Quarterly,* 66, 1 (2016), pp. 222–38.
Luisi, A., 'L'opposizione sotto Augusto: le due Giulie, Germanico e gli amici', in M. Sordi (ed.) *Fazioni e congiure nel mondo antico* (Milan 1999), pp. 181–92.
Luisi, A., 'Ovidio e la corrente filo-antoniana di opposizione al regime', in M. Sordi (ed.) *L'opposizione nel mondo antico* (Milan 2000), pp. 181–94.
Luttwak, E., *The Grand Strategy of the Roman Empire: From the First Century A.D. to the Third* (Baltimore 1979).
Malloch, S., 'The end of the Rhine mutiny in Tacitus, Suetonius and Dio', *Classical Quarterly,* 54 (2004), pp. 198–210.
Mercogliano, F., *Pisone e i suoi complici. Ricerche sulla cognitio senatus* (Naples 2009).
Millar, F., *A Study of Cassius Dio* (Oxford 1964).
Millar, F., 'Ovid and the *Domus Augusta*: Rome seen from Tomoi', *The Journal of Roman Studies,* 83 (1993), pp. 1–17.
Mogenet, J., 'La conjuration de Clement', *L'antiquité classique,* 23, 2 (1954), pp. 321–30.
Montanari Caldini, R., 'Aspetti dell'astrologia in Germanico', in G. Bonamente and M. Segoloni (eds) *Germanico. La persona, la personalità, il personaggio* (Rome 1987), pp. 153–72.
Newbold, R., 'Social Tension at Rome during the Years of Tiberius' Reign', *Athenaeum,* 52 (1974), pp. 110–43.
Nichols, J., 'Antonia and Sejanus', *Historia: Zeitschrift für Alte Geschichte,* 24, 1 (1975), pp. 48–58.
Oliver, J. and Palmer, R., 'Text of the *Tabula Hebana*', *The American Journal of Philology,* 75, 3 (1954), pp. 225–49.
Paladini, M., 'La morte di Agrippa Postumo e la congiura di Clemente', *ACME: Annali della Facoltà di lettere e filosofia dell'Università degli studi di Milano,* 7, 3 (1954), pp. 313–29.
Pani, M., 'Osservazioni intorno alla tradizione di Germanico', *Annali della Facoltà di Magistero dell' Università degli Studi di Bari* (1966), pp. 107–20.

Pani, M., 'Il circolo di Germanico', *Annali della Facoltà di Magistero dell' Università degli Studi di Bari* (1968), pp. 109–27.

Pani, M., *Roma e i re d'Oriente da Augusto a Tiberio* (Bari 1972).

Pani, M., 'Seiano e gli amici di Germanico', *Quaderni di storia*, 5 (1977), pp. 135–46.

Pani, M., 'La missione di Germanico in Oriente: politica estera e politica interna', in G. Bonamente and M. Segoloni (eds) *Germanico. La persona, la personalità, il personaggio* (Roma 1987), pp. 1–23.

Pani, M., 'Memoria dei Cesari e organizzazione del "nuovo *status Rei Publicae*", in A. Fraschetti (ed.) *La commemorazione di Germanico nella documentazione epigrafica* (Rome 2000), pp. 201–19.

Pani, M., *La corte dei Cesari da Augusto a Nerone* (Bari 2003).

Panvini Rosati, F., 'La monetazione di Germanico nel quadro della politica monetaria Giulio-Claudia', in G. Bonamente and M. Segoloni (eds) *Germanico. La persona, la personalità, il personaggio* (Rome 1987), pp. 79–86.

Pelling, C., 'Tacitus and Germanicus', in T. Luce and A. Woodman (eds) *Tacitus and the Tacitean Tradition* (Princeton 1993), pp. 59–85.

Pettinger, A., *The Republic in Danger: Drusus Libo and the Succession of Tiberius* (Oxford 2012).

Piattelli, S., 'Le legende monetarie di Germanico', in G. Bonamente and M. Segoloni (eds) *Germanico. La persona, la personalità, il personaggio* (Rome 1987), pp. 87–93.

Potter, D., 'The *Tabula Siarensis*, Tiberius, the Senate, and the eastern boundary of the Roman Empire', *Zeitschrift für Papyrologie und Epigraphik*, 69 (1987), pp. 269–76.

Potter, D. and Damon, C., 'The *Senatus Consultum de Cn. Pisone Patre*', *The American Journal of Philology*, 120, 1 (1999), pp. 13–42.

Powell, L., *Germanicus: The Magnificent Life and Mysterious Death of Rome's Most Popular General* (Barnsley 2016).

Powell, L., *Marcus Agrippa: Right-Hand Man to Caesar Augustus* (Barnsley 2023).

Questa, C., 'Il viaggio di Germanico in Oriente e Tacito', *Maia* (1957), pp. 318–48.

Questa, C., 'Sallustio, Tacito e l'imperialismo romano', in *Publio Cornelio Tacito: Annali* (Milan 2010), pp. V–LIV.

Rivière, Y., *Germanicus: Prince Romain. 15 av. J.-C. – 19 apr. J.-C.* (Paris 2016).

Roberto, U., 'Dopo Teutoburgo: Germanico sul Reno e i rapporti con Tiberio (11–14)', in A. Galimberti, R. Cristofoli, and F. Rohr Vio (eds) *Germanico nel contesto politico di età Giulio Claudia. La figura, il carisma, la memoria* (Rome 2020), pp. 5–25.

Rogers, R., 'The Conspiracy of Agrippina', *Transactions and Proceedings of the American Philological Association*, 62 (1931), pp. 141–68.

Rohr Vio, F., *Le voci del dissenso: Ottaviano Augusto e i suoi oppositori* (Padua 2000).

Rohr Vio, F., *Contro il principe: congiure e dissenso nella Roma di Augusto* (Bologna 2011).

Rose, C.B., *Dynastic Commemoration and Imperial Portraiture in the Julio-Claudian Period* (Cambridge, New York and Melbourne 1997).

Saladino, V., 'Iscrizioni latine di Roselle (III)', *Zeitschrift für Papyrologie und Epigraphik,* 40 (1980), pp. 229–48.

Salvo, D., 'Germanico e la rivolta delle legioni del Reno', *ὅρμος – Ricerche di Storia Antica*, 2 (2010), pp. 138–56.

Schulz, V., 'Historiography and Panegyric: The deconstruction of Imperial Representation in Cassius Dio's Roman History', in C. Lange and J. Madsen (eds) *Cassius Dio: Greek Intellectual and Roman Politician* (Leiden 2016), pp. 276–95.

Seager, R., *Tiberius* (London 1972).

Severy, B., 'Family and State in the Early Imperial Monarchy: the *senatus consultum de Cn. Pisone patre, Tabula Siarensis* and *Tabula Hebana*', *Classical Philology*, 95, 3 (2000), pp. 318–37.

Shotter, D., 'The Trial of Gaius Silius (A.D. 24)', *Latomus,* 26, 3 (1967), pp. 712–16.

Shotter, D., 'Tacitus, Tiberius and Germanicus', *Historia: Zeitschrift für Alte Geschichte,* 17, 2 (1968), pp. 194–214.

Shotter, D., 'The Trial of Clutorius Priscus', *Greece and Rome,* 16, 1 (1969), pp. 14–18.

Shotter, D., 'The Trial of M. Scribonius Libo Drusus', *Historia: Zeitschrift für Alte Geschichte,* 21, 1 (1972), pp. 88–98.

Shotter, D., 'The Fall of Sejanus: Two Problems', *Classical Philology,* 69, 1 (1974), pp. 42–6.

Shotter, D., 'Cnaeus Calpurnius Piso, Legate of Syria', *Historia: Zeitschrift für Alte Geschichte,* 36, 2 (1987), pp. 229–45.

Shotter, D., 'Agrippina the Elder: A woman in a man's world', *Historia: Zeitschrift für Alte Geschichte,* 49, 3 (2000), pp. 341–57.

Smith, R., 'The imperial reliefs from the *Sebasteion* at Aphrodisias', *The Journal of Roman Studies,* 77, pp. 88-138.

Sordi, M., 'Introduzione', in *Cassio Dione: Storia Romana – volume sesto* (Milan 1999), pp. 5–23.

Sordi, M., 'La morte di Agrippa Postumo e la rivolta di Germania del 14 d.C.', in M. Sordi (ed.) *Scritti di storia romana* (Milan 2002), pp. 309–23.

Spinosa, A., *Tiberio: l'imperatore che non amava Roma* (Milan 1988).

Starr, R., 'The Scope and Genre of Velleius' History', *The Classical Quarterly,* 31, 1 (1981), pp. 162–74.

Storoni Mazzolani, L., *Tiberio o la spirale del potere* (Milan 1981).

Sumner, G., 'The Truth about Velleius Paterculus: Prolegomena', *Harvard Studies in Classical Philology,* 74 (1970), pp. 257–97.

Suspène, A., 'Germanicus: les temoignages numismatiques', *Cahiers du Centre Gustave Glotz,* 24 (2013), pp. 175–95.

Sutherland, C. and Carson, R., *Roman Imperial Coinage. Volume I* (London 1984).

Syme, R., *The Roman Revolution* (Oxford 1939).

Syme, R., *Tacitus* (Oxford 1958).

Syme, R., 'Mendacity in Velleius', *The American Journal of Philology,* 99, 1 (1978), pp. 45–63.

Syme, R., 'Governors dying in Syria', *Zeitschrift für Papyrologie und Epigraphik*, 41 (1981), pp. 125–44.

Timpe, D., *Der Triumph des Germanicus. Untersuchungen zu den Feldzügen der jahre 14–16 n. Chr. in Germanien* (Bonn 1968).

Traina, G. and Buongiorno, P., 'L'*imperium* di Germanico, l'Armenia e l'Oriente', in A. Galimberti, R. Cristofoli and F. Rohr Vio (eds) *Germanico nel contesto politico di età Giulio Claudia. La figura, il carisma, la memoria* (Rome 2020), pp. 99–122.

Tuplin, C., 'The False Drusus of AD 31 and the Fall of Sejanus', *Latomus*, 46, 4 (1987), pp. 781–805.

Valentini, A., '*Rapere ad exercitus:* il bienno 14–16 d.C. e l'opposizione a Tiberio', in R. Cristofoli, A. Galimberti and F. Rohr Vio (eds) *Lo spazio del non-allineamento a Roma fra Tarda Repubblica e Primo Principato. Forme e figure dell'opposizione politica* (Rome 2014), pp. 143–65.

Valentini, A., *Agrippina Maggiore: una matrona nella politica della domus Augusta* (Venice 2019).

Wallace-Hadrill, A., *Suetonius: The Scholar and his Caesars* (London 1983).

Weingärtner, D., *Die Aegyptienreise des Germanicus* (Bonn 1969).

Weinrib, E., 'The family connections of M. Livius Drusus Libo', *Harvard Studies in Classical Philology*, 72 (1968), pp. 247–78.

Williams, K., 'Tacitus' Germanicus and the Principate', *Latomus*, 68, 1 (2009), pp. 117–30.

Winterling, A., *Caligula: A biography* (Berkeley 2011).

Wishart, D., *Germanicus* (London 2002).

Yavetz, Z., *Tiberio: dalla finzione alla pazzia* (Bari 1999).

Index